CLAUDE AKE MEMORIAL PAPERS NO. 12

FEDERAL SOLUTIONS TO STATE FAILURE IN AFRICA

By Eghosa E. Osaghae

UPPSALA
UNIVERSITET

Indexing terms:

FEDERALISM
STATE
POLITICS
GOVERNANCE
STATE COLLAPSE
AFRICA

Cover photo: Mogadishu, Somalia, August 2012. A Burundian officer serving with the African Union Mission in Somalia (AMISOM) gestures with a Somali man in front of a war damaged building.

Photo: Stuart Price, AU-UN IST

Federal Solutions to State Failure in Africa
Claude Ake Memorial Papers No 12

© 2020 Nordiska Afrikainstitutet/The Nordic Africa Institute, Institutionen för freds- och konfliktforskning vid Uppsala universitet/University University Department of Peace and Conflict Research, and the author

Author: Eghosa E. Osaghae

ISSN 1654-7489
ISBN 978-91-7106-866-8   print-on-demand version
ISBN 978-91-7106-867-5   pdf e-book

Language Editor: Clive Liddiard
Layout and Production Editor: Henrik Alfredsson

The Nordic Africa Institute conducts independent, policy-relevant research, provides analysis and informs decision-making, with the aim of advancing research-based knowledge of contemporary Africa. The institute is jointly financed by the governments of Finland, Iceland and Sweden.

The opinions expressed in this volume are those of the author and do not necessarily reflect the views of the Nordic Africa Institute.

CONTENTS

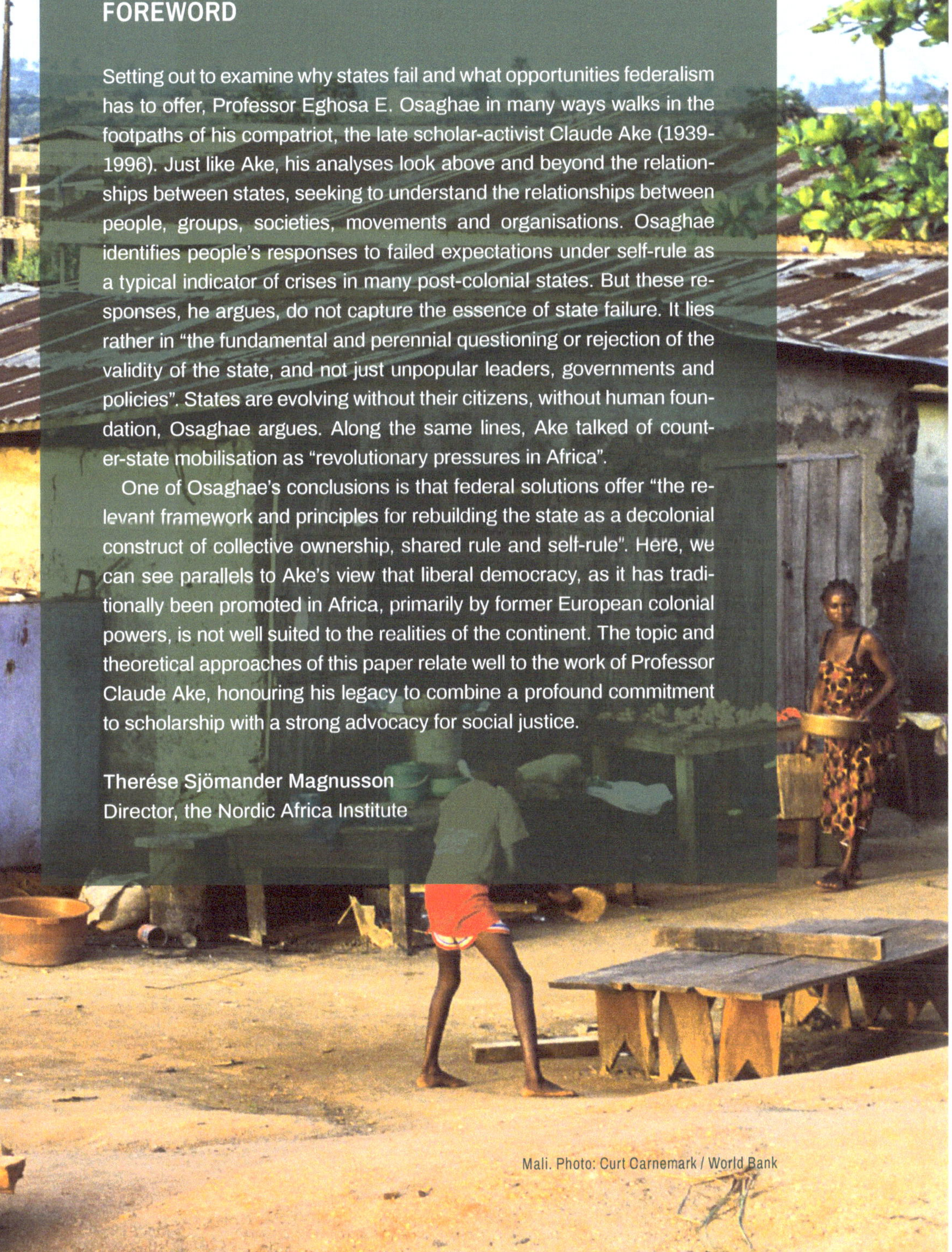

FOREWORD

Setting out to examine why states fail and what opportunities federalism has to offer, Professor Eghosa E. Osaghae in many ways walks in the footpaths of his compatriot, the late scholar-activist Claude Ake (1939-1996). Just like Ake, his analyses look above and beyond the relationships between states, seeking to understand the relationships between people, groups, societies, movements and organisations. Osaghae identifies people's responses to failed expectations under self-rule as a typical indicator of crises in many post-colonial states. But these responses, he argues, do not capture the essence of state failure. It lies rather in "the fundamental and perennial questioning or rejection of the validity of the state, and not just unpopular leaders, governments and policies". States are evolving without their citizens, without human foundation, Osaghae argues. Along the same lines, Ake talked of counter-state mobilisation as "revolutionary pressures in Africa".

One of Osaghae's conclusions is that federal solutions offer "the relevant framework and principles for rebuilding the state as a decolonial construct of collective ownership, shared rule and self-rule". Here, we can see parallels to Ake's view that liberal democracy, as it has traditionally been promoted in Africa, primarily by former European colonial powers, is not well suited to the realities of the continent. The topic and theoretical approaches of this paper relate well to the work of Professor Claude Ake, honouring his legacy to combine a profound commitment to scholarship with a strong advocacy for social justice.

Therése Sjömander Magnusson
Director, the Nordic Africa Institute

Mali. Photo: Curt Carnemark / World Bank

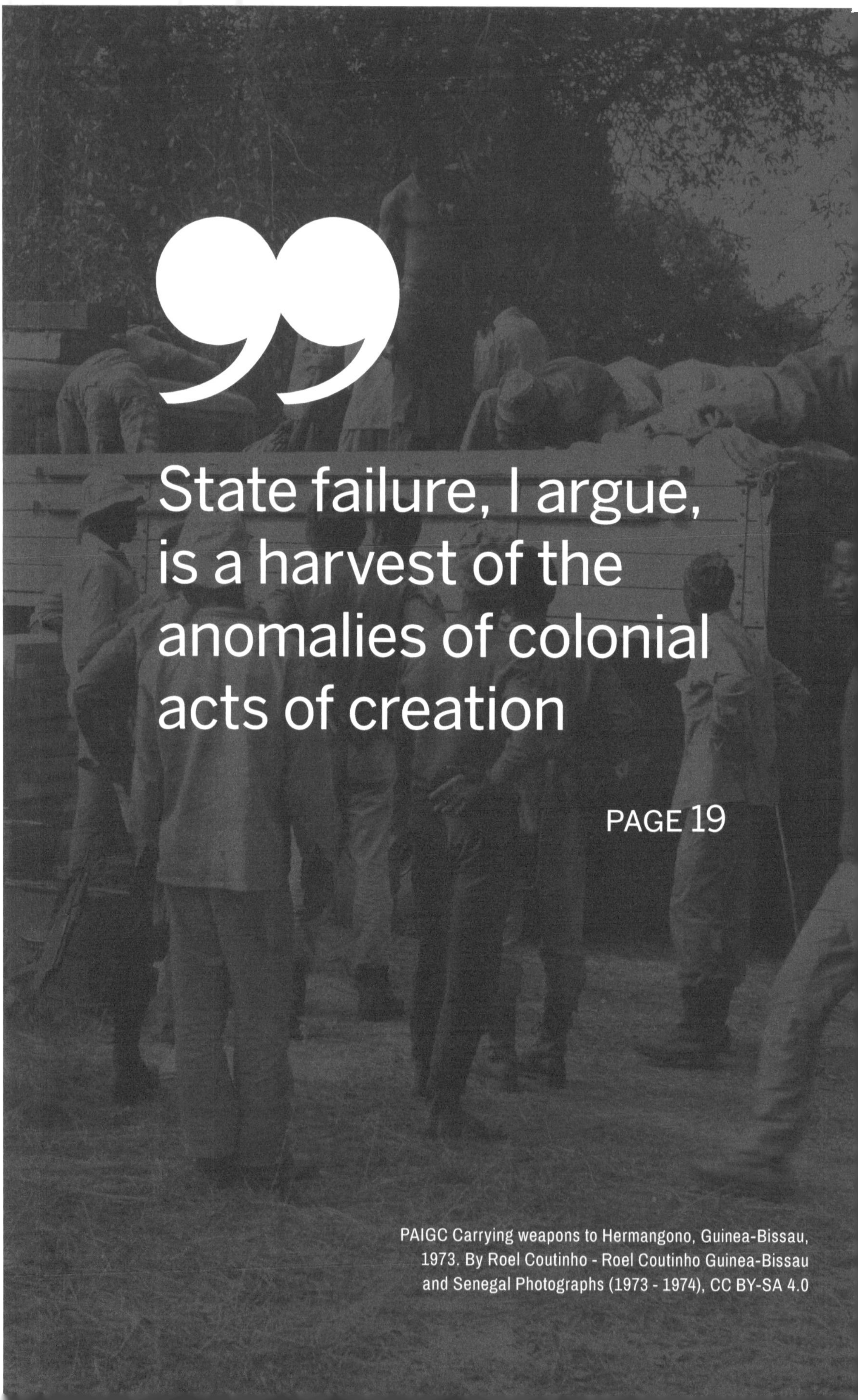

State failure, I argue, is a harvest of the anomalies of colonial acts of creation

PAGE 19

PAIGC Carrying weapons to Hermangono, Guinea-Bissau, 1973. By Roel Coutinho - Roel Coutinho Guinea-Bissau and Senegal Photographs (1973 - 1974), CC BY-SA 4.0

INTRODUCTION

Scholarly interest in the study of federalism in Africa has increased in recent times, although it remains low, relative to overall interest in the subject of federalism (cf. Erk and Swenden, 2010). This is probably because many share Burgess' conclusion that 'Federalism in Africa does not have a positive image. Its record of success is patchy, while its failures seem manifest' (Burgess 2012a:3, also see Burgess, 2012b). The methodological errors in such thinking should be immediately obvious. First is the implied selection bias of choosing only cases that support, or are positive about, federal theory and practice; and second is the unwillingness to consider that 'federalism in Africa' could represent a different variety or genre of federalism, in much the same way as we think of 'Anglo-Saxon', 'continental European' and 'American' traditions and varieties of comparative federalism (Osaghae, 1997; Watts, 2013; Hueglin and Fenna, 2015). The latter error shows how normative thinking that expects federalism everywhere to conform to a particular – even if supposedly universal – model limits understanding of its rich variety. A similar limitation applies to the more generic concept of state, which is also usually presented in a universalistic cast. Issues like these are germane to my concerns in this paper, for reasons that will become clear as we go on.

At this point, it is sufficient to note that, fortunately, such issues have not prevented analysis of the utility of federal solutions in the management of diversity, minority problems and governance from including African cases in considerations of the significance, applicability, potentials and limitations of federalism (Erk, 2014). The extensive application of decentralisation (which is regarded with qualification as a variant of federalism, Osaghae, 1990) as a tool of governance and political reforms in Africa where according to Wunsch 'it has been undertaken in more countries than anywhere else in the world' (Wunsch 2014:1), is a case in point (also see Suberu, 2013; Dickovick and Wunsch, 2014; Erk, 2014). This interest has not waned because decentralisation has failed to strengthen governance at the local level, as expected – paradoxically it has strengthened the central state and disempowered local governments in many countries (Dickovick and Wunsch, 2014; Stren and Eyoh, 2007) – but it's unintended consequence has rather helped to explain why decentralisation is not a one-size-fits-all solution, and why it does not always work. This ought to be the case with federalism and the state, where they (federalism and the state) fail to conform to or fit into universal categories and the attendant expectations. The point cannot be overemphasised that here are important lessons to be learnt from the failure of models or systems, because more often than not failure shows the possibility of a *false universal* or, simply put, that universal models do not apply or work everywhere (Wiredu, 1996).

As a legal-constitutional system of government of fairly rigid rules and practices, federalism in Africa might not have a positive image, but the overall relevance and utility of federalism for state-building on the continent has been grossly underesti-mated, for reasons related to narrow legal-constitutional standards. Suberu (2013) acknowledges the 'tremendous appeal, resonance and relevance' of federal ideas and institutions across the continent's 54 states, but – like many other scholars – feels obliged by legal-constitutional lenses to raise doubts about their capacities to be truly federal. Insights from more expansive sociological and political perspec-tives, which relate federal solutions to the underlying social formations that drive federal practices and outcomes, suggest, however, that the forces of federalism are more compelling and relevant to state-building and consolidation processes in Africa than has generally been acknowledged. This is the perspective that I wish to explore in this paper. The long history of floundering statehood, of dissatisfaction and rejection of it by critical segments of those groups around which citizenry is ordered, has provoked the question of how viable artificial' and 'imposed' states, in which constituents have yet to resolve the basis of belonging together, are. States may be 'accidents of history' and 'geographical expressions' – as indeed many are; but the trajectory of state formation in Africa that involved the arbitrary delineation of boundaries, naming and lumping together of groups many of which were rein-vented in the acts of colonial creation, is a road not well travelled.

A PROBLEM OF COLONIAL IMPOSITION

The situation of the state in Africa is not simply another instance of managing the challenges of diversity in multinational or multicultural states – challenges that many of the world's countries face today, especially with the unprecedented rise of iden-tity politics. Unlike multinational states in Europe and North America, for exam-ple, which have shared political cultures and traditions of statehood, and therefore have some consensual basis for staying together, many states in Africa were formed by forcibly amalgamating different groups that lacked shared traditions or histories; there was consensus on statehood and citizenship. These groups are simply obliged to belong to and operate within state categories over which they have no control, having been excluded as subjects rather than citizens in the construction of the states (Mamdani, 1997; Ayoade, 1988). This has been at the heart of the problem of the state – the so-called national question in Africa. But what exactly is the nature of the problem? Is it a problem of colonial imposition, at whose core lies, accord-ing to Ekeh (1983), social structures imported wholesale from the Mother Colony – structures with little or no indigenous or local underpinning, and whose exogenous origins, orientations and interests have continuously affected their legitimacy and effectiveness? Is it a clash of civilisations? Or is it a problem of cultural incompati-bility and resistance to encounters with modernity? It could very well be any (or all) of these, as has been argued by Bayart (1991, 1992), who believes that statehood in Africa has been mostly deviant; but the question of what to do with malformed states and social formations has not been seriously addressed. The recent and ongoing debates provoked by the crisis of the state – of which state failure in Africa is a variant – present an opportunity to fundamentally address this lacuna, as state failure raises questions about the tenability of supposedly universal state models in Africa.

Contrary to what the dominant ahistorical narratives on the subject suggest, state failure is neither simply the failure of institutional capacity (or the weakness of institutions) nor a consequence of African pathologies (neo-patrimonialism, corruption, ethnicity, despotism, etc.): rather, it indicates that the inherited state forms in Africa – with all their limitations – have failed to work, have finally unravelled and have fallen apart. Some contributors to the debate agree with this interpretation of state failure (see especially Scott, 2017), but stop short of insisting on rebuilding the state, as opposed to saving, revamping and reforming it. One exception is Wunsch (2000), who not only makes a strong case for refounding the African state, but makes that process contingent on the application of federal and consociational systems (as we do in this paper). Though Wunsch does not specifically refer to state failure, the weak foundations of local governance and ownership that he analyses are integral to failure. Others who recognise the need to rebuild, reconstitute and reconstruct the state for reasons of the coloniality of power and the imperative of second independence, however, operate outside the failed state debate (Nzongola-Ntalaja, 1987; Ndlovu-Gatsheni, 2015; Agbese and Kieh, 2007). Suberu (2013: 27) is spot on when he observes that the issue of territorial legitimacy 'has generally been avoided in Africa where the prevailing norm is to maintain existing state boundaries at all costs, rather than to accept their negotiability or reversibility through democratic processes'; but he also falls short of suggesting what to do, despite recognising the abundant relevance of federalism to Africa.

Both 'rebuilding the state' and 'saving the state' are within-state options that accept the sanctity of extant territorial boundaries and composition; but while 'saving' presupposes legitimacy and functionality, and means reaffirming and strengthening the state in its flawed condition (or literally flogging a dead horse, in top-down arrangements), 'rebuilding' implies giving the state new, inclusive and more assured foundations, both to correct the anomalies of colonial acts of creation and to make the states more acceptable, legitimate and viable. This is not, however, to be confused with the narrower (and fleeting) context of rebuilding states after protracted conflict and war. Even though post-conflict situations may be regarded as offering some of the best instances of state-building (as countries like Rwanda and Somalia have shown), the emphasis on short- to medium-term solutions – typically donor aid and investment, infrastructural renewal, transitory power-sharing arrangements and constitutional reforms – may not go far enough in addressing the structural imperatives necessary to remedy the anomalous colonial foundations of the state, unless they are transformed into sustainable and enduring structures.

Rebuilding involves reconfiguring the state on the basis of a desire on the part of constituent groups to be its collective owners, while at the same time exercising some control over matters that are best managed by them. This has a ring of familiarity: *majimboism* or the more recent *ugatuzi* – both variants of devolution and regionalism in Kenya and several other countries (Ghana, Uganda, Tanzania, Senegal and Zimbabwe) – local government reform, and the recent and ongoing wave of decentralisation across the continent aimed at creating various degrees of local autonomy all spring immediately to mind. These arrangements have arisen partly in response to local demands, and partly as a consequence of donor-driven governance reforms; but they have mostly been undertaken according to the narrative of 'saving the state', and therefore at the behest of the central state, in typical top-down fashion. State rebuilding, by contrast, revolves around a more negotiated process of central (national) vs non-central (subnational) engagement, rather than around central unilateralism; this allows constituent groups a (guaranteed and continuous) say, and gives them a sense of belonging at both the national and the subnational level. It involves a more extensive use of federal solutions, though not necessarily in the legal-constitutional sense of full-fledged federal government. Studies framed in the legal-constitutional mould mostly dwell on the deficits of critical political, economic and institutional capacities that constrain federalism and decentralisation in Africa, and on their failure to meet the normative and ideal standards of 'universal' federalism in the legal-constitutional mould (Suberu, 2013; Boone, 2003; Chanie, 2007); but we find better and more appropriate applications of the principle in the way in which federal solutions – in the more expansive and nuanced sense – can be used to refound the state, and perhaps, in the process, set federalism itself on a trajectory that works, especially in solving those constitutive problems that lie at the core of state failure.

TRADITIONS OF NEGOTIATED AND INCLUSIVE STATEHOOD

The case for federal approach(es) to state rebuilding can be justified on a number of grounds. *The first* is that traditions of negotiated and inclusive statehood are fairly well grounded in historical narratives across Africa. Several precolonial states had diversities that were carefully managed through reciprocal relationships that enabled kings and kingdoms to mobilise armies for common defence, and economies and social cohesion to grow on the basis of a division of labour and mutual exchanges. The oft-cited dispersal of territories – which allowed communities, including vassal states and groups separated by geographical barriers to enjoy considerable autonomy in core-periphery arrangements (Herbst, 2000) – was a key factor here. On the political front, the Ashanti confederacy, Benin, Mandingo and several Yoruba states operated as political, economic and military alliances, and power sharing and balances were institutionalised in many societies, including supposed-

Students in Brewerville, Liberia, March 2012. The school was built for the Sande Society in Liberia. Photo: Travis Lupick.

ly 'stateless' societies (Eisenstadt et al., 1988). The Poro (men's) and Sande (women's) societies that spread across several groups – including the Bassa, Gola, Kissi, Vai, Mende, Limba and Kono in present-day Liberia, Sierra Leone, Guinea and Ivory Coast – mastered the norms of alternating political and ritual control of land and complementary economic and social roles in order to further inclusive cohesion. The trajectory of dispersed authority and local autonomy continued under colonial rule – especially in the practice of indirect rule, which recognised established local jurisdictions of territorial authority. Indeed, colonial constructions of tribal identities were tied to territorial ownership, and notions of homelands, hometowns and autonomous communities with sharp indigene/non-indigene differentiations has endured as the major diacritic for characterising ethnic groups in the thick of the 'politics of belonging' (Geshiere, 2013; Osaghae, 1986). Thus, the Ethiopian constitution defines (ethnic) nations, nationalities and peoples as groups that (i) have common culture, language or religion, and (ii) constitute identifiable territory.

At the most generic level, communalism and social exchange reciprocities enabled and sustained cultures of accommodation of difference. So, the federal dimensions of indigenous formations were both territorial and cultural, and these continue to be reflected in contemporary expectations that object to the politics of exclusion and domination. They also resonate in the strong traditions of local autonomy and self-help development, by which several groups claim ownership of and participation in decision-making that affects their lives. These traditions often serve as necessary levers for negotiating intergroup relations. Finally, the idea of African despots and authoritarian tendencies – the popular typification of African authority and political culture which some scholars regard as one of the disenablers of federalism – was largely a colonial creation and belongs to Ekeh's (1983) category of transformed social structure: that is, indigenous institutions and practices that were reinvented (in mainly adverse ways) to serve the purposes of colonialism.

POPULAR OPTIONS FOR HOLDING STATES TOGETHER

The second reason for federal approaches and solutions is that they are popular options for holding states together in Africa, even if they have not always worked as expected (Gana and Egwu, 2003). For colonisers, federalism provided an expedient strategy for meeting their core economic and political objectives: it helped to consolidate control of large and diverse territories and to ensure that colonies paid for themselves through amalgamations that enabled well-endowed territories to subsidise poorer territories. These were the key objectives of the colonial Federation of Rhodesia and Nyasaland, the British East African Federation, Federation d'Afrique Occidentale Francaise, Federation d'Afrique Equatoriale Francaise, and Africa Orientale Italiana. What these federations had in common was that they were 'negotiated' by the colonial authorities of the elements, which came together without any reference to the African peoples of the territories. The Nigerian federation, which emerged from the amalgamation of the Northern and Southern Protectorates at the time, followed a similar trajectory, leaving the Union of South Africa (1910) – which arose with the unification of the Transvaal, Cape Colony, Natal Colony and Orange River Colony – as the only voluntary and self-determined colonial federation. The unequal exchanges of the larger colonial federations were a major source of tension, and led to their eventual collapse (see, for example, the debates between Leopold Senghor of Senegal and Felix Houphouet-Boigny of Ivory Coast over the breakup of the Federation d'Afrique Occidentale Francaise and other disagreements, in Hazlewood, 1967). Colonial regimes also laid the foundations for, and oversaw the adoption of, federalism in Nigeria, Uganda and Kenya.

At independence, when the danger of possible disintegration loomed large, the federal formula was in great demand and was often applied; and it certainly helped to hold together Nigeria, Uganda, Kenya, Cameroon, Ghana and – much later – Ethiopia, South Africa, Congo, the Comoros, Somalia, Sudan and South Sudan (after the two countries separated). The case of countries with dual or mixed colonial inheritances, whose territories had been ruled by more than one colonial power and were subsequently amalgamated into single countries – Cameroon (Francophone and Anglophone), Ghana (British Togoland and Gold Coast), Somalia (Italian and

British) – is particularly noteworthy in this regard. So, also, are territorial delineations of ethnic, religious, economic, geographic and social diversity, which create de facto asymmetries that often require deliberate balancing and equitable policies to ameliorate them. Large size and divided territory, as in Ethiopia and the Comoros, complete the picture. In Comoros, the archipelago of the four separate and semi-autonomous islands of Mwali (Moheli), Maore (Mayotte), Ndzuwani (Anjouan) and Ngazidja (Grand Comore) made a federal arrangement somewhat inevitable (although the status of the Island of Mayotte which is a French Overseas Department is highly contested by the Comoros which claims it as part of the Union of Comoros).

These were the circumstances that led to the adoption of federal constitutions, devolutionary and regional arrangements, and ethnic arithmetic formulas of power sharing in various countries. The initial designs did not last long in countries like Uganda, Cameroon and Kenya that ended up with federal constitutions, because the ruling elites (which regarded a federal arrangement as a pragmatic means to an end, rather than as an end in itself) preferred the short-cut unicentre option of one-party rule. Nonetheless, the arrangements did advance the cause of national integration (Smock and Bentsi-Enchill, 1976) and helped to hold the states together in the critical period of uncertainty – and even afterwards, as federal considerations remained prominent on the agenda of political discourse, in the demands for restructuring and redress, and in the periodic bargains struck in those countries (as exemplified by the *majimbo* and *federo* movements in Kenya and Uganda, respectively, in the 1990s). The demands for federal solutions and instrumentalities did not abate after the first wave and the reversals of the 1960s. Rather, it has increased in relevance and application, pushed (as it were) by the unsettling waves of transition, conflict and war that have taken their toll on the state and resurrected the famous national question in several countries (Wunsch, 2000; Osaghae, 2004a, 2004b, 2005a). In South Africa, federalism proved a successful model for managing the transition to an inclusive post-apartheid state; in Ethiopia, it was adopted to accommodate the competing claims of the ethnic-based liberation movements; and in Kenya, it was remodelled in response to demands for regional autonomy. Federalism has also emerged as a popular choice for conflict management and post-conflict settlement and state reconstruction in Somalia, Sudan, South Sudan, DR Congo, Comoros, Liberia and Sierra Leone.

UNDEREXPLORED COMPLEXITY OF IDENTITY CATEGORIES

Thirdly, the somewhat peculiar (adaptive, experimental) circumstances of federalism in Africa, and the problems it has had to deal with, have led to the development of fairly innovative instrumentalities that enhance its utility for managing and re-building the state (this point is well acknowledged by scholars like Dent, 1989 and Horowitz, 2007, as Africa's contribution to the theory and practice of federalism).

A major part of this has to do with the often unacknowledged and underexplored complexity of identity categories in Africa. It is commonplace to explain political problems in Africa – state-threatening mobilisations, conflicts, war, instability, electoral violence, democratic and governance deficits, etc. – as problems of ethnicity and ethnic differences, and the assumption is that ethnic groups are organic and fixed, as integral to Africa's inherent tribalism. But this is far from the reality: many of the ethnic groups in contemporary Africa may have their origins in pristine or precolonial formations, but their present forms (size, language and territory, especially) and their relations with one another owe a lot to colonial acts of creation, which involved the classification and profiling of natives. Some of the groups were, in fact, the product of administrative restructuring and linguistic classification; but they all evolved within the new colonial states, and have been in the throes of construction and reconstruction ever since. Ethnic identities and division have nevertheless shown a great deal of resilience through structures of traditional authority, legal pluralism (mixes of common law mostly inherited from colonial masters, customary law and Islamic law, and multiple conflict-management structures) and elite politics to uphold systems of 'mixed government' or 'dual authority' (Owusu, 1983; Sklar, 1993, 1999). Traditional authority, in particular, is not only a major source of moral authority and social order in everyday life – the abode of the 'uncaptured peasantry', whose lives are guided by the economy of moral affection (Hyden, 1980); it also makes accommodation of difference imperative, because traditional polities rarely aspire to independent statehood (Sklar, 1993). Mixed government is further reinforced by customary law, which is entrenched all over Africa (though only a few countries – Mozambique, Botswana, Ghana and Uganda – have formally recognised it). All these elements have provided the 'resources' for identity constructions and reconstructions. Elsewhere, I have made the point that the simultaneous processes of ethnic construction and state construction provide the federal situation in Africa with one of its unique distinctions – malleability (Osaghae, 2019). As a result, Africa's federalism has been highly flexible, lending support to Livingston's (1952) hypothesis about the inherent capacity of federal instrumentalities to respond to the dynamics and changing demands of federal societies. Even for usually rigid institutions of federal government, Horowitz (2007: 103) makes the argument for flexibility – or deviation from the model US federal system – in a slightly different way: 'Whatever the design, outside of the United States, the configuration of institutions is not regarded as an unchangeable feature of the landscape but an arena of purposive activity in which the aim is to engineer institutions that can cope in a democratic way with the problems particular societies present.' It is instructive that, in presenting the Nigeria Independence Bill to Parliament in July 1960, the British secretary of state for the colonies, Mr Iain Macleod, made a point of reminding his colleagues that the federal constitution of Nigeria was not designed to 'be a rigid one'.

That said, some of the instrumentalities developed in Africa are eclectic and defy rigid federal-unitary divides (Suberu, 2013). One of the more notable is the elevation of local government as a third order of federalism, with constitutionally guaranteed powers and revenues. Nigeria pioneered this trajectory of federal theory and practice on the African continent, after Marshal Tito's Yugoslavia became the first federal system to make local government a separate tier of administration in the search for ways to optimise the scope for political accommodation in that country; it has since been joined by South Africa. Another method is 'the grant[ing] of autonomy to territorial subunits … [to] empower or appease ethnic minorities, transforming them from national minorities to subnational majorities' (Suberu, 2013: 26; also see Osaghae, 1998). This strategy is especially important on a continent where majority groups have held sway and pushed minorities into political *containment*; in contrast to political *accommodation*, this has relegated them to second-order belongingness at both the national and the subnational level (for this very useful differentiation, see Busia, 1967). Faced with the likelihood of state capture by dominant majorities, against all the odds Nigeria, Ethiopia and (to some extent) South Africa and Tanzania under Nyerere made appreciable efforts to reinvent minorities as subnational majorities; they offer important lessons for states with serious minority problems (see Horowitz, 2007, for an elaboration of how 'Madisonian methods' have been used to ameliorate problems of majoritarian rule in Africa and elsewhere). Other adaptive and innovative instrumentalities include the creation of legislative councils for traditional authorities; filling Ethiopia's House of the Federation (its upper legislative chamber) with representatives of nations, nationalities and peoples (rather than of component states), in order to underscore the point of collective ownership (for similar reasons, South Africa's equivalent is called the National Council of Provinces); devising an electoral system that blends a simple majority with geographical distribution (Nigeria); the adoption of multiple official languages (South Africa); and the creation of models of executive power sharing and elite coalition of the Government of National Unity variety, which have featured prominently in post-conflict peace-building and reconstruction. One might even add the secession clause that was adopted in Ethiopia, as a necessary safety valve to smooth the high-stakes bargaining among the ethnic-based liberation movements during Ethiopia's difficult transition (Habtu, 2005). It is instructive that at its most uncertain juncture of consensus-building among conflict groups, Sudan followed the Ethiopian lead by including a secession clause for South Sudan in its 2005 Comprehensive Peace Agreement, which ended decades of civil war. These innovative and experimental devices offer ready models and alternatives for rebuilding the state, especially in the light of Suberu's (2013: 26) observation that 'unitary arrangements do not typically provide for the representation of subnational authorities in the machinery of the central government'; this has been a major source of legitimacy problems in many states.

Poster celebrating the founding members of the the Organisation of African Unity (OAU) in 1963. They following year (1964), the OAU adopted the principle of stability of borders, uti possidetis, would be applied across the continent.

THE STABILITY-OF-BORDERS PRINCIPLE

The fourth and final factor justifying a federal solution is that the political mobilisations and demands for ownership, local autonomy, a shared central state and self-determination are mostly within-state. The stability-of-borders principle of *uti possidetis* in international law, which the Organisation of African Unity adopted in 1964 to retain/uphold colonial boundaries inherited at independence, set the initial framework for this. It is remarkable that despite the turbulence, conflict and wars on the continent, the colonial boundaries have remained largely intact, notwithstanding the fact that the boundaries 'represented the triumph of the European definition of the non-European world' (Scott, 2017:21). With the exceptions of Eritrea and South Sudan (which broke away from Ethiopia and Sudan, respectively), the secessionist and separatist agitations of Southern Cameroons and a few groups in Nigeria, such as the Indigenous People of Biafra (IPOB), the more recent demands and agitations accept the sanctity of state boundaries and are for more equitable, representative and collective ownership reconfigurations. This is true of even the more extrteme against-state mobilisations, such as terrorism and civil wars, which have been mostly triggered by domestic grievances. In relatively stable and peaceful situations, expanding political spaces and democratisation have led to claims and demands for inclusivity and equity rights by several groups, especially marginalised minority and resource-bearing groups. These have opened up spaces for state refoundation.

It is against the backdrop of the foregoing that I analyse the relevance and applicability of federal solutions to rebuilding the state in Africa, following its failure as a colonial construct. State failure, I argue, is a harvest of the anomalies of colonial acts of creation, especially the imposition of a dominant, received and supposedly universal state cast, which pays scant regard to autochthonous foundations or bearings. Once a state has unravelled, having reached the limits of its anomalous foundation and proven to be incapable of effective functioning in its present shape, the question is how it can be rebuilt in a manner that makes constituent groups and citizens its real owners – a consideration that ought to have informed its construction in the first place. This is the challenge of state failure; and I believe that federalism – in its most inclusive genus of belonging/holding-together solutions – provides a strategic framework for responding to it. (I should quickly point out that at this stage in Africa, the 'coming-together' or 'aggregative' species of federalism is less likely at the level of the state than it is at the level of regional and sub-regional integration, where it has been applied). Holding-together federalism (in effect, state-level federalism) offers contending (claimant, aggrieved, nationalist and rebellious) forces – in some cases for the first time ever – a platform for developing payoff matrices in bargaining strategies that can guarantee a measure of self-governance and a foothold (belongingness, share, ownership) in the central state. This is the setting for states that are commonly owned – unlike current state forms that allow the central state unilaterally to determine ownership and that have continually alienated, excluded and marginalised huge segments of the citizenry ever since their colonial establishment. The rest of the paper is structured as follows. In the next section, I interrogate the meanings and ramifications of state failure in Africa in greater detail. The section that follows does the same for federal solutions in their expansive federalism-without-federal-government forms. Then comes an analysis of the specific features of federal solutions to state failure in Africa. The final sections present the conclusions and acknowledgements.

State failure is a consequence of the fact that the contemporary African state is 'neither African nor state'

Page 27

A column of ONLF rebels during the Somalia war, September 2006.
Photo: Jonathan Alpeyrie

STATE FAILURE

The major point of departure for this paper is the debate provoked by what has come to be known as state failure in Africa. State failure is, of course, not peculiar to Africa: states have fallen and failed throughout history and all over the world. But African state failure is quite unique, as it marks the failure of the dominant, established and supposedly universal state form that was grafted onto Africa through colonial acts of creation. It is not a case of physical collapse or ruin, but of states that subsist and continue to exist and be recognised for what they essentially are not.

The anomalous foundations of the colonial state and its successor that are at the root of failure are fairly well established in the literature, but surprisingly they have received scant attention in the scholarship on state failure in Africa, in which failure is largely attributed to institutional weakness and other endogenous factors. This perception of state failure clearly mistakes effect for cause, since it omits to locate state failure in the flawed – and contested – foundations of the state. For this reason, I would argue, the dominant perspectives on state failure – which allude to crisis in governance and capacity weakness – are inadequate for recasting the state in the required fundamental ways. A fixation with upholding existing state paradigms, following the one-size-fits-all framework – reinvented by the regime-change agenda of neoliberal hegemony, in what Ndlovu-Gatsheni (2015: 3) calls a 'postcolonial neo-colonised world' – means that the dominant perspectives are incapable of drawing the important lessons and implications of state failure in Africa for the comparative study of the state as a generic construct. And the main lesson is that the paradigm does not work in all situations. (For precisely the same reason, Horowitz, 2007 criticises those American scholars of federalism who refuse to analyse the frontiers of federalism beyond the US model). The African experience shows why this is so, and how relevant varieties which fit African conditions and peculiarities can be built. It is necessary to state right at the outset that the case being made is not for an alternative state form that is uniquely African, in the sense of being culturally specific or different (even though political cultures, being building blocks for political formations, including states, do set states apart). The international order of sovereign central or nation states is here to stay. Even precolonial formations in Africa and Asia gravitated towards the central state, long before their integration into the current order (although it should be noted that the anthropological and historical narratives that shaped the classifications of precolonial systems into state/stateless categories in Africa, for example, were based on European precepts). The problem is not that the central state is here to stay, but that the modern order, 'a standard of civilisation', is highly Eurocentric (Scott, 2017: 11). Indeed, state forms were reimagined to make them correspond to European conceptions of statehood, so that even those states like Ethiopia and Liberia that managed to resist colonisation 'had to assert their rights to statehood in terms of the criteria set in Europe' (Scott, 2017: 13). Be that as it may, one of the major points I hope this paper makes is that there are many paths to state-building, and states have the right to adopt the path that suits them.

The term 'state failure' has generally been used to refer to the inability of state structures and institutions to work as they are expected to, and to deliver on the major functions of statehood in the areas of integration, governance, stability, human security and development (Osaghae, 2007). The indices of failure – or what many scholars like to refer to as crisis (see the contributions in Lewis and Harbeson, 2016) – are well known and include perennial instability, endemic legitimacy problems, contested citizenship, frequent challenges to the authority of the central state, prevalence of forced rather than voluntary compliance in areas of in areas of citizen obligation (like payment of taxes and compliance with laid down rules and regulations), prevalence of exit from the state to shadow states, illegal migration and the rise of separatist and militant groups. But what exactly do these things mean, and what is the nature of the crisis? What does it mean, for example, to say that a low (or non-existent) capacity for conflict management is a state-failure variable, when the legitimacy of the very state itself is contested? Are Lewis and Harbeson (2016: 3) right to imply that 'crisis indicates a chronic, deep-seated challenge of security, governance, or economic viability' that arises from multiple sources of vulnerabilities – emergencies, unexpected wars, political upheaval, social violence and uneven economic performance – without interrogating the sources of the vulnerabilities? State failure has also been framed in terms of its consequences – disorder, conflict, war and collapse. Chabal and Daloz (1999) attempted to rationalise disorder, suggesting that it was more a neo-patrimonial instrument for coping with political crisis, than an indicator of failure; but they clearly underestimated the character of state failure that gave rise to neo-patrimonialism. It is a degenerative process that can be accelerated by shocks and sparks, such as violent elections or economic decline; but it is not caused by them, and failure is persistent and not episodic. In the light of the confused – and what I consider to be mistaken – applications of the concept, it is necessary to clarify the meaning and ramifications of state failure.

THE ORIGINS OF FAILURE

Beginning with the pioneering work of Jackson and Rosberg (1982) on why Africa's weak states persist, state failure has been approached mainly as an empirical construct. The parameters follow the Westphalian and Weberian criteria for statehood – territory, population, government, economy and sovereignty. Jackson and Rosberg found that many states in Africa were empirically weak (having unstable territories and populations, and ineffective governments that did not have a monopoly on legitimate force and were too dependent to be sovereign), and only survived on the shoestring of juridical recognition as states under international law. Since Jackson and Rosberg's time, many weak states have come to swell the ranks of fragile and failed states, whose defining elements have broadened out to include other pathologies, like corruption, economic insolvency, infrastructural decay, capital flight, human rights abuse, and threats to global peace and security as sources of illegal migration, human trafficking, the modern slave trade, terrorism, cross-border conflicts, drugs, cybercrime, etc. Defined in these terms, the reality of state failure and its unsavoury consequences cannot be denied, but how to deal with them? There have been two broad responses. The first attributes failure to empirical structural and institutional weaknesses and deficits, implying that failed states can be made to work again if the appropriate therapies are applied (Chesterman et al., 2005; Lewis and Harbeson, 2016). This line of thinking stands in sharp contrast to the second (and far less sympathetic) response, which includes overseeing the demise and possible takeover of failed states as trusteeships or civil society holdings in the initial stages (Clapham, 2001, 2011; Herbst, 2004; Bates, 2008). As far as the proponents of the latter perspective were concerned, failed states in Africa were no better than 'legal fictions' – 'little more than a pretence, maintained by the international system because it lacks any intellectual or legal framework other than statehood through which to understand and cope with developments on the ground' (Clapham, 2011:82). This hardline perspective also encompassed a benign variant of self-colonisation, advanced by leading African social theorist Ali Mazrui (1995) and not unexpectedly criticised by fellow African scholars as something done 'in the service of imperialism' (see Mafeje, 1995, 1998; Bangura, 1995).

For hardliners like Clapham, failed states had become dispensable because they subsisted as 'parasites' and 'unacceptable burdens' on the rest of the world, and were 'incapable and unwilling to mend their ways' (Kothari, 1988: 4–5). In the end, the more hopeful and positivist perspective – which was prepared to give failed states another chance – won through. It received an important conceptual boost from the burgeoning neo-institutional approaches in comparative politics, which, in response to the larger crisis of the state, brought formal and informal institutions of state, including constitutions, back in as the main units of analysis of post-behavioural methodological reconstruction (Steinmo et al., 1992; Weaver and Rockman 1993; Peters, 1999; Pierson, 2000; Kuperman, 2015). The institutional focus has been further boosted by the development of so-called evidence-based perspectives of international development agencies, donors and practitioners, which also accept that state remediation can be effected through interventions of (mostly short-cut) regime change reforms in governance that hinge on measurable templates of institutional change (Helman and Ratner, 1992–93; Rotberg, 2004). Decentralisation and reform of key governance structures (constitutions, legislatures, judiciary, local government, fiscal and monetary policies, etc.) whose success depends largely on donor support are some of the more popular interventions.

The bigger problem, however, is that as a construct, state failure also carries normative connotations. First and foremost, it signifies the failure of extant states in Africa to live up to the expectations and ideals – the 'conventional indicators of economic performance and governance' (Lewis and Harbeson, 2016: 3) – that define statehood in the dominant Western paradigms in which they have their origins. Simply put, state failure implies deviance from and non-conformity to accepted standards (or, as some milder references have it, global best practices of political organisation). Sometimes this is simply non-conformity that threatens Western interests, values and hegemony – a situation that warranted the de-legitimation of countries that the US called rogue states. For this reason, the dominant state-failure literature locates both state-building and remediation in the hands of those who have patented the state model and provided the banisters of its construction, and reduces the entire process to learning and practising more of what is required to make received state paradigms work (Boas and Jennings, 2007). To this extent, Scott (2017: 27) is right in her observation that studies of failed states 'favour solutions over understanding'.

This is a rough sketch of the normative frame of state failure, but it shows how partial and one-sided the narratives are. What are the narratives from the failed states themselves? First, state failure is not new: it is as old as the beginnings of the modern states in Africa – in fact, the notion of failure is embedded in, and original to, states established by colonial imposition. In other words, it is in the colonial constructions that we find the origins of failure. As Scott (2017: 21) puts it, 'it is the condensation of imperial forms of subjugation and the consequent universality of statehood that underscores the problematics of contemporary state failure'. This is as much from the point of view of the peoples of the state, as it is of the structural disabilities and weaknesses of the colonial state. With regard to the former, several accounts point to the disconnection between the colonial state and the peoples who were alienated from the state (see especially, Mamdani, 1997). The state deprived the subject peoples of their rights, and failed either to protect them or to further their welfare in significant areas, thereby forcing them to create parallel states (mostly in the form of self-help improvement associations and tribal unions) that delivered public goods (vigilantes, primary and secondary schools, health centres, scholarships, postal agencies, earth roads, and so on) that the state failed to provide. Missionaries also played a major parallel-state role, especially in the provision of educational and healthcare facilities. Whatever elements of state welfare existed were reserved for the few Europeans, especially in the settler colonies. Although major corrections and advances have been made since independence in social infrastructure and service delivery – to the point where people now expect the state to do virtually everything for them – the basic disconnections remain. They explain why, for example, transparency and accountability in the public realm remain thin, and why citizens would rather shield criminals than report them to the police, as many

Congo Balolo Mission School, ca 1889-1891. Missionaries also played a major parallel-state role, especially in the provision of educational and healthcare facilities. Unknown photographer.

people still view government and the state with suspicion and misgivings fit only for alien structures. The structural disabilities can be summarised by the empirical fact that colonial states were mostly quasi-states, as the empirical bases of states were tenuous, fragile and undeveloped. Boundaries were blurred and, in some cases, indeterminate; government bureaucracy was minuscule (except, of course, for the army and police, which were overdeveloped); 'citizen' obligation was coerced; and infrastructure was restricted to key areas of the colonial economy. Moreover, from the foundations laid by the forerunner colonial companies, the colonial state institutionalised the logic of extraction, which promoted infrastructural development as essentially for revenue extraction, rather than for the welfare of citizens and the common good, and which gave the state control over major resources, including land, which was expropriated from the people. This logic of extraction, which dispossessed local people of their resources and denied them the benefits of their yields, was widely accepted as a 'working model' by the political elite that governed the countries after independence, in their bid to build a material power base.

RESPONSES TO FAILED EXPECTATIONS

There is some consensus among analysts of political formations in the post-independence era in Africa that, with a few notable exceptions, the post-colonial state retained the trappings of the colonial state, especially in its relations with its citizens and constituent groups. The following characterisation of a dysfunctional state in 2006 could as easily describe the colonial state of the preceding paragraph: '[the state lacks] provision of welfare and opportunity to the population' (Herbst and Mills, 2006: 1). In essence, independence turned out to be merely a shift of power from foreign to native hands, and therefore failed to meet the expectation that it would be 'a transformation of the whole pattern of political life, a metamorphosis of subjects into citizens' (Geertz, 1963: 104). This was the beginning of the wide gulf that ensued between the 'revolution of rising expectations' (such as the promises of a better life fuelled by independence, election campaigns and new governments) and the 'revolution of rising frustrations' that came in the wake of continued failure to meet the expectations and a deterioration in material conditions. Rather than prosperity, there was deprivation, unemployment and poverty; and rather than freedom, security, equity and fairness, there was exclusion, marginalisation, injustice, insecurity, suppression and denial of rights. Of course, none of this was new, having been embedded in the character of the colonial state; but such failings were inexcusable under self-rule, and provoked the frustration, withdrawal of support, contestation and counter-state mobilisation that Ake (1987) rightly sums up as 'revolutionary pressures in Africa'.

Responses to failed expectations – such as periodic electoral defeats of, or protests against, bad leaders and governments, for example – can also pass as typical indicators of crisis, but they do not capture the essence of state failure sui generis. That essence lies rather in the fundamental and perennial questioning or rejection of the validity of the state, and not just unpopular leaders, governments and policies. Separatist agitations, intractable conflicts, wars and even terrorism are some of the more dramatic and extreme manifestations of these tendencies, but they are also inherent in day-to-day acts of dissociation, such as refusal to pay taxes or obey rules and regulations, opportunistic and instrumentalist relations that approach the state only in terms of pillage and benefits, and warlike elections that take the form of violent referendums on state legitimacy, rather than competitions for power. Of these various manifestations of state failure, none seems as pervasive as the failure to make the state and managers accountable. It has become evident that accountability cannot be possible when the legitimacy of the state itself is questioned. Terrorism, arguably the most extreme form of anti-state mobilisation, presents an interesting case. Contrary to popular views that tie terrorist activities to global impulses and movements, the motivations for hardline terrorist groups in Somalia, Kenya and Nigeria have come more from local grievances and demands for state reconstitution interests, than from global causes to which they have been circumstantially related (Menkhaus and Shapiro, 2010; Osaghae, 2020). This has led to the conclusion that 'contested states rather than failed states are generally the sites of terrorism' (Newman, 2007). In essence, state failure signifies the inappropriateness of extant states, their configurations, orientations and objectives, and manifests itself in the demands of citizens and constituent groups for their reconstitution on the basis of self-determined precepts to serve popular interests and demands. (This is similar to what Nzongola-Ntalaja, 1987 calls the transformation from the colonial state to a 'people's state'; also see Agbese and Kieh, 2007, and Ndlovu-Gatsheni, 2015, for a further elaboration of the state reconstitution thesis.) The demands, as noted earlier, are not for new states as replacement states, but for a rebuilding of existing states.

To sum up, state failure is a consequence of the fact that the contemporary African state is 'neither African nor state' (Englebert, 1997). In the words of Scott (2017: 25) it is 'less the failure of existing states and more the failed rooting of imported and reified models of statehood – models which developed out of a particular set of circumstances in European societies and which should not necessarily be viewed as the zenith of sociopolitical organisation and appropriate everywhere'. It is to the historically located 'failed rooting' that we must turn to remedy state failure (Ellis, 2005), and doing so involves transforming the state from its colonial and supposedly universal cast, to an organic state, freely negotiated and owned by the peoples and constituent groups on the basis of self-determination.

The juncture of state failure presents a historical moment to apply federal solutions in more fundamentally enduring ways

Page 33

FEDERAL SOLUTIONS

One aspect of federalism that tends to be underplayed is the fact that it is a strategy of state-building and statecraft that is adopted either at the inception of the state (we shall call this 'inception-state federalism'), or later, when the need arises to rebuild, reconfigure or reinvent the state (we call this 'later-state federalism'). Inception-state federal systems, best exemplified by the USA, Switzerland and other old and mature federations, were established through the coming-together or aggregation of autonomous political units, which desired to have common government for some shared purposes (mostly related to defence in the initial stages), but to retain self-rule in areas of difference.

In Africa, the only notable cases of inception-state federalism have been: Tanzania, a union formed in 1964 by Tanganyika and Zanzibar under the Articles of the Union; the Mali Federation, which was a pan-Africanist experiment by Senegal and the then French Sudan (now Mali); and the East African Federation, with Kenya and Uganda as the prime movers. Of these, only Tanzania has survived. More recent examples of aggregative unions are provided by sub-regional economic and political unions, such as the Economic Community of West African States (ECOWAS) and the Southern African Development Community (SADC), and the African Union, the new pan-African grouping (though these are more confederal than federal).

Later-state federal systems that fall under Horowitz's (2007) category of devolution federalism began as unitary states, which were later disaggregated to give the component units varying measures of self-rule and shared rule for the purposes of holding the state together as a single entity (after it became obvious that unitary arrangements could not serve this goal). Countries with fledgling, unstable and contested statehood constitute the bulk of these – especially states forcibly moulded by colonial acts of creation; others where diversities and insular identities are politicised and accentuated by demands for separation, self-determination, representation and inclusivity; and countries threatened by majoritarian rule or torn apart by conflict and war. The large (and expanding) number of such countries – which now include microstates that long ago would not have been considered eligible for a federal system (because it was believed that large size and population were necessary conditions for federalism) – has extended the significance and use of federal solutions. Veenendaal (2015) shows that all 20 of the smallest UN member states, with populations ranging from 10,000 (Nauru) to 197,000 (Samoa), have some variety of local administrations and other complexions of federalism. African cases would include Liberia, Sierra Leone, Benin, Togo and Guinea-Bissau, which have tiny populations or territories, but where federal solutions of the power-sharing and decentralisation variety have been applied. The essence of later-state federalism was captured long ago by Livingston, who argued that 'As the nature of society changes, demands for new instrumentalities are created and these demands are met by changing or abolishing old instrumentalities and establishing new ones in their places' (1952: 93). What the many examples of later-state

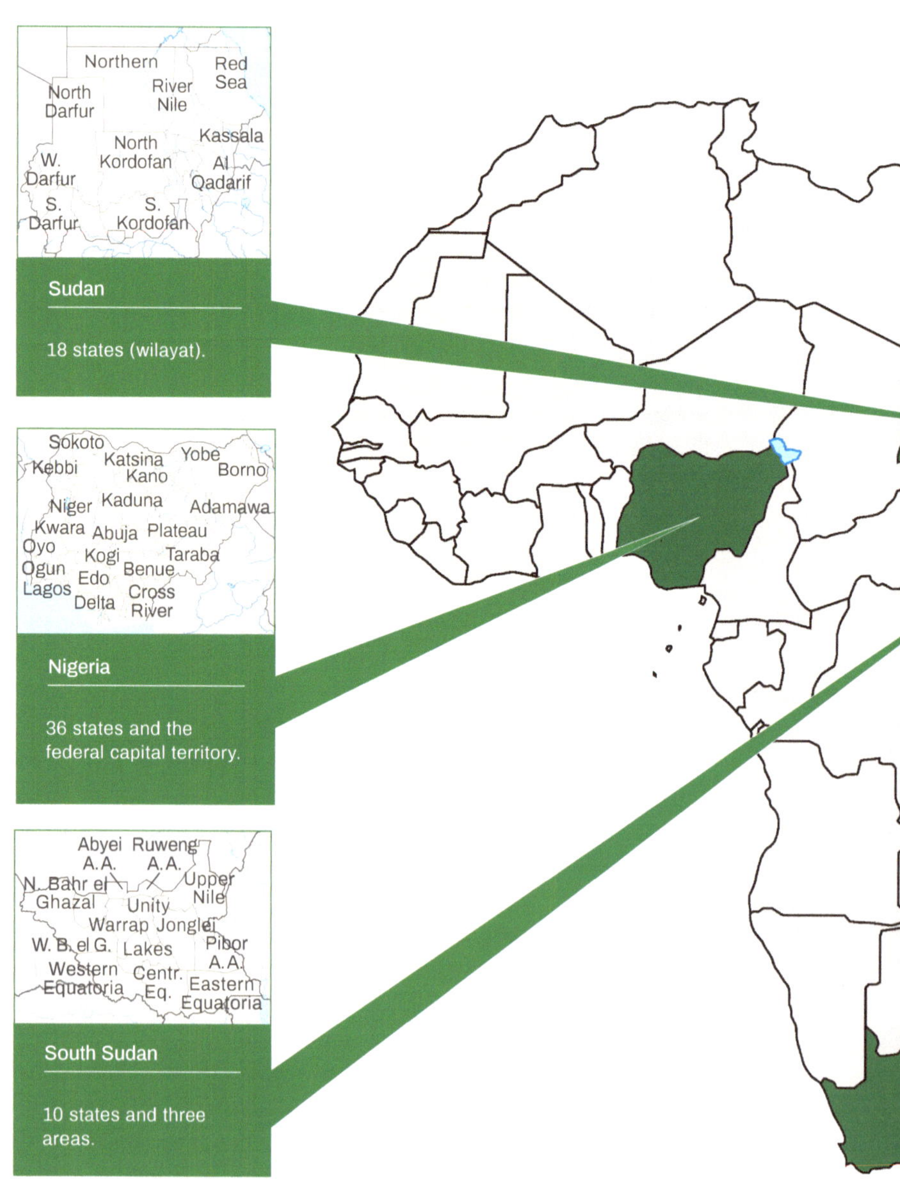

federalism show – and which is germane to the thesis of this paper – is that federal solutions are not synonymous with federal government, and that any such equation restricts the scope of federal approaches to state-building.

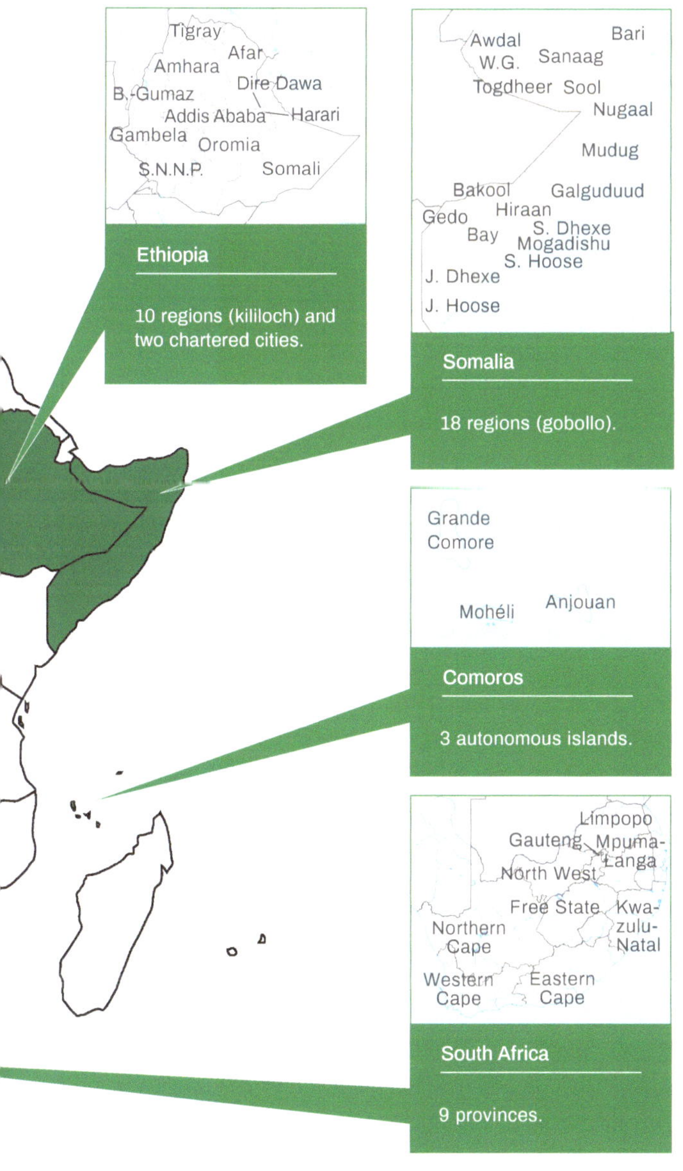

Federal states in Africa. Defining which states are federations, devolutions or merely decentralised is of course a delicate academic task. South Africa, for example, is by some scholars defined as a unitary state, by others as a de facto-federation. This map-based compilation is by no means to be seen as an effort to enter into the highly contested definition domaine, it merely serves as an illustration of the seven African states that are constitutionally federal, including the contested case of South Africa.

This point becomes clearer when we consider another important difference between inception-state federalism and later-state federalism. Inception-state federalism is generally more legal-constitutional and thoroughgoing as federal government in which power is shared between the central government and the constituent units in such a way that (i) each level of government has matters on which it takes the final decisions, and (ii) no level of government can unilaterally change the terms. Here, federalism is both a means to an end and an end in itself. Purist federal scholars like Wheare (1967) insist that this is the true definition of federalism; but it is too restrictive in terms of the essence and range of federal solutions, and certainly cannot account for the many countries that apply them. By contrast, arrangements in later-state federalism are more flexible, expansive, creative and even informal, and are driven more by sociological forces than by legal-constitutional strictures. This makes each later-state federal solution more a means to an end than an end in itself. Later-state federalism presents a wider variety of federal solutions that constitute the category I have referred to elsewhere as federalism-without-federal-government. A distinctive feature of this is the heuristic application of federal principles (agreement, consensus, common ownership, and simultaneous self-rule and shared rule) to diversity management and other problems of governance (Osaghae, 1997).

The significance of this variety is that a country or political system does not have to be a federation, or to operate a federal constitution or government, in order to be regarded as applying a federal solution (which, as I have said, is more a means to an end than an end in itself). Federalism-without-federal-government takes several forms, including territorial and non-territorial power-sharing arrangements (such as regional or local autonomy and decentralisation), executive power sharing, a rotational presidency, affirmative action, reverse discrimination, and such elements of consociationalism as non-majoritarian democracy, proportionality, minority veto, a quota system and segmental autonomy, all of which entail one or more elements of common ownership, consensus, self-rule and shared rule (Lijphart, 1985). Countries with thoroughgoing federal constitutions and governments – like Nigeria, Ethiopia and South Africa (which also happen to be some of the more divided) – are not, of course, excluded from these more pragmatic uses, as they have invented or adopted various additional federalism-without-federal-government instrumentalities, like a rotational presidency, executive power sharing, a quota system, multiple national languages, and affirmative action to enhance the efficacy of the federal formula. In relatively less-divided countries, elite power sharing, inclusive multicultural arrangements and decentralisation generally suffice, although the possibility of growing to become thoroughgoing federal systems cannot be ruled out. The point, however, is that in almost all cases, practices that would be considered unfederal in thoroughgoing federalism – such as over-centralisation and secession clauses – are excusable (for 'strict' federal principles, see Wheare, 1967; and see Dent, 1989, for the 'excusables'). This flexibility is what has made federal solutions attractive and widely applicable in later-state federalism.

LESS POTENT WHEN APPLIED LATE

While the relevance of federalism as a problem-solving (in this case state-building) device is well acknowledged, Horowitz believes that timing is a critical factor in the efficacy of federal solutions in later-state or devolution federalism. According to him, federal solutions tend to become less effective or potent when applied late, typically 'when conflicts have progressed to a seriously disintegrative or violent stage':

> It then becomes a matter of the central government's yielding a great deal of power to the substate units, often simply to facilitate the ability of ethnic contestants to live in separate compartments while purporting to inhabit a common central state. (Horowitz, 2007: 105)

Kimenyi (1997) makes a similar point in relation to conflict situations in Africa. So, when is the most appropriate time for federal solutions? Early on, says Horowitz, when the opportunity to make a serious choice, such as independence or re-democratisation, presents itself. This does not always guarantee success – witness the African cases of Uganda, Cameroon and Kenya, whose federal constitutions were abrogated shortly after independence; however, the federal solution at least helped to keep those countries together. One case that lends support to the timeliness thesis has to be South Africa, whose 'miraculous' transition to the post-apartheid state in the face of threats of disintegration owed much to the adoption of federal principles in the bargains struck and agreements reached by the leaders of the African National Congress, National Party, Inkatha Freedom Party, Freedom Front, the nominally independent homelands of Transkei, Venda, Bophuthatswana and Ciskei, and other major political groups. Horowitz believes that Sri Lanka could have been spared the agony of its deadly and prolonged civil war, had a federal solution been adopted early on. The same can be said for the Democratic Republic of Congo, Sudan and Somalia, which turned to federalism a little late in the day, and for Cameroon, where the intransigence of President Paul Biya over demands by aggrieved Anglophones for the restoration of the federal system forced the separatists to take up arms and declare independence in the two southern regions. For the purposes of this paper, we would say that the juncture of state failure presents a historical moment to apply federal solutions in more fundamentally enduring ways.

Federalism is a system of continuous bargaining

Page 37

FEDERAL SOLUTIONS TO STATE FAILURE

Let us now turn to the specific matter of federal solutions to state failure. By federal solutions we mean a collection of formulas and arrangements that entrench and continuously promote agreement, consensus and common ownership as cornerstones of the state, and that involve degrees of simultaneous self-rule (the possibility that autonomous decisions and actions can be made in certain matters) and shared rule (the possibility of participation and representation in decisions and actions affecting the country as a whole). Although solutions are to be understood as providing answers to problems, they are not 'cures' in themselves, but 'structured context[s] within which ... [the problems] may be confronted' (McKown, 1988: 298), and 'a means to encourage ongoing social exchange when simple inclusion in government is not sufficient because of the divergent interests of various groups' (Thomas-Woolley and Keller, 1994: 414). To set a proper framework for discussing the application of federal solutions to state failure, two points that were made earlier should be re-emphasised. The first is that federal solutions are familiar terrain in Africa; the second is that federal solutions do not require those states that employ them to be federations or to have federal governments. A third caveat is also necessary. This is that the use or appropriateness of federal solutions is determined by contextual factors and specificities relating to political culture, political economy, history, nature of diversity, character of elite, party system, and so on. In other words, they are not one-size-fits-all solutions; and even though they entail common and general principles and instrumentalities, countries have to work out the solutions that best suit their circumstances. As Shridath Ramphal, former secretary-general of the Commonwealth, put it long ago:

> The practical necessities of a miscellany of national circumstances, not the symmetry of academic reasoning have given [federalism] its content and form ... Federalism does not require that countries must mould their institutions to immutable principles or forms of organisation. It promises instead, that federal constitutions may be designed to meet the particular needs of the communities establishing them. (Ramphal, 1979: xiv)

But how are federal solutions arrived at? Who is involved in their development and adoption? And how does applying federal solutions to rebuild the state differ from managing diversity, which is the more familiar terrain in the literature (Rothchild,

1997)? It is easy to think of federalism as some kind of rational response to the objective circumstances of ethnic, cultural, territorial and religious diversity – in other words, to imagine that situations of diversity invite federal solutions. Not only does such a line of thought ignore the fact that diversity is a necessary but not sufficient factor for federalism (not all diverse countries apply federal solutions, and especially not of the thoroughgoing federalism species), but it also leads to the assignment of responsibility for adopting federal solutions to central states, as part of their integrative functions. At least, this was how the British, in particular, embraced the federal formula to manage the affairs of their large and diverse colonial states; and indeed, many of those who consider later-state federalism to be a device for managing diversity think likewise.

This is more so that the criteria for measuring the success of federalism in post-colonial states – including a reduction in violence and chaos (McKown, 1988), or national unity, democratic politics and socioeconomic development (Adamolekun and Kincaid, 1991) – are essentially central state efficiency variables. But the federal process is more complex than is suggested by such a one-way-traffic or top-down rational-choice formulation. For one thing, the perspectives of non-central state actors or claimants – a necessary part of the federal matrix – often paint a different and conflicting picture. According to McHenry, 1997: 6), minorities and other federalism-seeking groups are likely to judge success by the extent to which federalism maximises the groups' freedom and autonomy'. Rothchild (1999: 323) makes a similar point when he lists the following as conditions under which minority nationalists (or any other ethnic nationalists, for that matter) are more likely to cooperate with central state elites:

> (1) demands are negotiable; (2) the state is responsive to legitimate demands; (3) the perceptions of state elites are pragmatic; (4) authentic representatives of the main ethnic groups are included in the decision-making process; and (5) there are no hurtful or antagonistic political memories.

Given the simultaneous opposing centripetal and centrifugal forces, the demands and processes that lead up to a federal solution involve multi-layered negotiations and bargaining among several actors: mainly central states and claimant constituent units or groups, but also political organisations, rights-seeking groups, militias, rebel groups and warlords; in the African context, many of these have emerged from the disruptions of state failure. According to Thomas-Woolley and Keller (1994: 414), 'Federalism provides negotiating mechanisms to establish workable patterns of interaction between the state and the various groups themselves.' In the final analysis, it is to be expected that the nature of federal solutions – and especially the degrees of self-rule and shared rule in whatever form – will be a reflection of the bargains struck by constituents at a given point in time, since federalism is a system of continuous bargaining.

Once again, the bargaining element is more apparent in inception-state federal systems, which in the first place are products of voluntary bargains among previously autonomous units. It is no less required in later-state federalism systems, especially when the aim is to rebuild the state through renegotiation of its foundations; but it is a much more difficult process. Dudley (1966: 92) provides one explanation for this:

> In older federations, the stresses generated [by bargains] tend to be ameliorated by established rules which limit the permissible boundaries of bargaining. In newer federations, such rules are often non-existent since the rules themselves are a product of recent bargaining situations.

A more important reason is the reluctance of powerful and integration-minded central states to reduce their power or share it with subnational units that they themselves have created. Countries that operate a federal government (Nigeria, South Africa, Ethiopia) may have fared better in this regard, to the extent that the adoption of federal constitutions was preceded by negotiations among key stakeholders – constituent subnational units, central government, political parties, liberation movements and civil society organisations – in transitional constitutional/ national conferences and constituent assemblies. But even in these cases – as groups that have demanded restructuring and true federalism in Nigeria since the 1990s have discovered – this has not made subsequent bargains over common ownership, self-rule and shared rule under asymmetrical conditions of an overbearing central government any easier.

In Cameroon, the separatist agitation in the southern regions by Anglophones who were seeking an end to Francophone domination – agitation that could have been halted by the restoration of federalism, as demanded by the separatists – resulted in armed struggle and a declaration of independence, simply because the central state dug its heels in and refused to negotiate with the aggrieved groups. The Anglophones in Cameroon are a minority, with only two (Northwest and Southwest) of the country's eight provinces. They allege that the national government treats them as an ethnic group ('tribe'), which they are not: they constitute several ethnic groups. They believe that they are marginalised, especially in the field of higher education, which is a facilitator of upward mobility and competitiveness (there is a long-standing demand for a 'proper' Anglophone university, the University of Buea being regarded as an outpost of the Francophone

Universities of Yaounde I and II). Grievances like this could be addressed through negotiation.

Thus, at different stages across the continent, the dominance of all-powerful central states (and of the leaders who personified them) either prevented or delayed the necessary reconstruction work. In several countries, it took a weakening of the central state and of the powerful rulers – or in some cases their defeat by competing forces – to change the power equation and open the doors to a renegotiation of the state. Insurrections, popular revolts, agitations for political restructuring and resource control, street uprisings, the rise of rights groups, electoral violence, terrorism, civil war, secessionist movements, etc. showed the way all over the continent. The Arab Spring, which triggered state-rebuilding protests in Tunisia, Algeria, Libya, Egypt and parts of the Middle East, emerged as a possible model, being more politically intense and more intent on regime change than the riots against the structural adjustment programmes (the 'anti-SAP riots') of the 1980s and 1990s that prefaced the democratic struggles in many countries; but elsewhere on the continent it had little impact. Sudan came closest to the Arab Spring model, as the 2019 uprisings there led to the overthrow of Omar Al-Bashir, who had ruled the country for three decades; to resistance to the takeover by military generals, who tried to hijack the situation; and ultimately to negotiations over how the state should be reconstituted. Thus, even though emergencies are not required (or even good) triggers for change – not least because they often get hijacked by opportunistic warlords and rebel leaders seeking short-term benefits – they do reflect fault lines and contending forces, reduce the scope for central state unilateralism, and offer opportunities for state-rebuilding bargaining.

NATIONAL CONFERENCES AND MULTIPARTY POLITICS

Among the less disruptive – even if still mostly forced – modes or platforms, the national conferences that emerged in the 1990s as a popular mode of democratic transition in Francophone countries (Benin, Togo, Congo, Zaire, Chad, Niger) served as default models for state renegotiation, as did multiparty politics. Heilbrunn (1993) recognises the strength of national conferences as stipulating 'norms of inter-group bargaining', but understates their significance and scope by analysing them only in terms of the pro-democracy mobilisations of civil society. The reaches of the transition mode as sovereign assemblies, whose resolutions are final and binding, are better captured by the Benin case:

> … the assembly of delegates that met during 19–26 February 1990 was supposed to be representative of all social, religious, professional, and political interest groups whose aim was to intro-

> duce a constitutional liberal democracy. This Conference nationales
> managed to gain acceptance of sovereignty which it had declared
> on the second day – namely, that all its decisions would be legal and
> binding. (Nwajiaku, 1994: 429)

Although a combination of factors – including the meddlesomeness of France, which worked to maintain the status quo of its former colony-states – made it difficult for the national conferences to attain their full potential as platforms for renegotiating the state, the facts that they were sovereign and that their decisions were legally binding made them attractive models for state-renegotiation champions, as they seemed to provide an antidote to the problem of overbearing central governments and autocratic rulers. Thus, for a long time national conference was the preferred mode of engagement and bargaining by groups demanding true federalism and restructuring in Nigeria and Cameroon. In Cameroon, the 'national dialogue' convened by the central state in 2019 issued important proposals, including the adoption of a special status for the two Anglophone regions and restoration of the House of Traditional Rulers and of the country's former name – the United Republic of Cameroon; but because it fell short of a sovereign conference (decisions reached were to be approved by the president), the dialogue was boycotted by separatist Anglophone groups. In Kenya, Ghana, Guinea, Ethiopia and Congo, referendums have also emerged as a popular model for building consensus and a sense of ownership of constitutions and administrative restructuring.

The return of multiparty and competitive politics, which opened up previously closed and suppressed spaces and saw alternations of power holding and the defeat of incumbents, also expanded the scope for bargaining. In some cases (such as Kenya), it took inconclusive elections and violent outcomes for this to happen. The resurrection of civil society and the rise of pro-democracy and rights groups also emboldened excluded and marginalised groups – including, most notably, ethnic minorities – to demand group and equity protection rights, and helped to set the rules for negotiating state reconstitution (Osaghae, 2000). Resource-control agitations also emerged as a key aspect of state renegotiation, with land-owning and resource-bearing groups – which, from colonial times, had been continually denied the benefits accruing from 'their' resources – seeking a say on (if not indeed total control of) how the rents, royalties and other revenue from minerals (oil, diamonds, gold) and other commodities were to be used.

These were the circumstances that propelled and hallmarked the state renegotiation movements, beginning with the second independence struggles of the late 1980s all across the continent (Osaghae, 2005b). The issues and demands of these movements – whose goals were to reduce central state unilateralism and tyranny, and ensure collective ownership of the state – included the following: guaranteed inclusivity and equitable representation and participation in the central state and its agencies; devolution of power to subnational units, with guaranteed measures of autonomy and self-rule; resource control and revenue access for constituent groups, both to support autonomy and to enhance equitable distribution; and guaranteed space for continuous expressions of self-determination, exchanges and bargains through democratic structures – human (individual and group) rights, competitive party politics, elections and constitutional rule.

POWER-SHARING PRACTICES

The evidence from across the continent is that, whatever the situation in which countries find themselves – whether they are engaged in relatively peaceful, post-conflict settlements and peace-building, or are literally having to rebuild themselves from scratch (Somalia, South Sudan) – these issues have elicited responses that are overwhelmingly based on federal principles. Perhaps the most widespread of these are the power-sharing practices that have become fairly well established in several countries. Some, like Ghana, Uganda and Kenya, have emulated Nigeria's 'federal character' principle. As a constitutional directive principle of state policy, this requires the country's 'federal character' to be reflected in the composition both of the federal government and its agencies and of subnational units, in order to promote a sense of belonging and prevent the domination of government at every level by people from one or a few groups. In almost all countries, increased sensitivities over issues of domination, exclusion and marginalisation have led to new formulas of rotational presidency, the zoning of top government positions, and power-balancing arrangements to ensure that the president, presiding officers of legislative bodies, chief justices, and the heads of the army, police and other agencies do not come from the same place. The scope and mechanisms of power sharing and shared rule have continued to expand. The 2005 constitution of the Democratic Republic of Congo created a Conference of Governors to give voice to the country's 26 provinces and to promote cooperative federalism between the national and provincial governments. The conference, which is chaired by the president, is mandated to ensure inter-provincial harmony and provide advice to the two levels of government.

The search for more meaningful shared rule and collective ownership has also involved extension of the representation and participation arena beyond the executive to the legislature. South Africa has developed the most elaborate framework in this area. The upper legislative chamber, the Council of Provinces, is constitutionally mandated to ensure that provincial interests are protected in the national government, especially in matters of provincial powers and boundaries, matters related to shared national and provincial legislative competences, and other specifically provincial matters, which cannot be amended without the approval of the council (this requires six of the nine provincial delegations to vote in favour). To further ensure the representation and protection of subnational interests at the national level, the council also has representatives of organised local government (South African Local Government Association), who have no voting rights but who are allowed to take part in debates.

Ethiopia has something similar, although membership of the upper chamber – the House of the Federation – is more 'organic': it comprises representatives of nations, nationalities and peoples, rather than of component states, in order to underscore the point of collective ownership, which recognises nations, nationalities and peoples as the true owners of the federation. The Democratic Republic of Congo has followed the legislative approach to shared rule: members of the Senate are elected directly by the provincial legislative assemblies. The adoption of multiple national languages and the granting of the right to language (including mother-tongue education), religion, culture and development – which imply group rights – have also enhanced the collective ownership infrastructure. Although issues have been raised about the capacity of many groups to develop local languages, for example, and to effectively assert this right (the case of Afar in Ethiopia discussed by Fiseha, 2012, provides a classic example), the recognition of several languages is significant, and marks a radical departure from the past, when the languages of dominant groups were imposed as a lingua franca. DR Congo has devised a useful strategy for making the languages count: all laws passed by the central state have to be published in all four national languages – Kikongo, Lingala, Tshiluba and Swahili – within 60 days. It has also been pointed out that South Africa supplements its 'rainbow' approach with a liberal approach, which expects that participation rights should promote integration without ethnification of politics (see Fessha, 2010).

It may be argued that what is outlined above represents some of the less complicated areas, to which federal solutions can easily be applied because central states have little or no difficulty in conceding ground on them. The more difficult issues are those that have to do with making concessions for the purpose of shared rule with subnational units: devolution and resource control. But before analysing these issues, let us consider a foundational structural issue: the manner of, or criteria for, disaggregating subnational units, which also has implications for determining who the true 'owners' of the countries are. The protocol established since colonial times has been for central states to create and split units on the basis of administrative convenience, 'natural' geographical boundaries and the preferences of elites with vested interests, but rarely on the basis of the wishes of the people. The constituent units are, as a result, as artificial as the colonial states themselves. Ethiopia has made deliberate efforts to resolve this dilemma as an ethnic federation. According to article 46(2) of the Ethiopian constitution, states are formed on the basis of settlement patterns, language, identity and *consent of the peoples concerned*. The secession clause and the right of peoples, nationalities and groups to establish their own states can be read as empowering this intent to give meaning to notions of self-determination and ownership. These are further reinforced in the constitutions of regional states. Article 39 of the amended constitution of the Southern Nations, Nationalities and Peoples Regional State (2001), for example, recognises the right of the nationalities and peoples of the state to secede and establish their own state, if the demand for this is approved by a two-thirds majority of members of the council of the area concerned, is presented to the state council, and is passed by a referendum. The referendum of 2019, in which the Sidama people voted overwhelmingly (98.5 per cent) for a state separate from the State of Southern Nations, Nationalities and Peoples, was an actualisation of what may be regarded as a fundamental group right.

But the problem of disaggregating subnational units is one that all later federal systems have had to deal with, because – for reasons that are partly to do with the marble-cake territorial patterns of ethnic identities and the often large numbers of groups desiring autonomy – it is almost impossible to have a perfect fit between the ethnic/linguistic/cultural/religious and the subnational unit. It has also been argued that creating subnational units on the basis of ethnic, linguistic and cultural affinities may be counterproductive, as this encourages the cultivation of discriminatory entitlements and privileges and ends up making the units the exclusive preserves of 'indigenes' and sons and daughters of the soil – closed, as it were, to 'non-indigenes', 'migrants' and settlers, as has been witnessed in Nigeria, Ghana, Uganda, Kenya, Cameroon and Ethiopia. But still, people and groups ought to have a say in the determination of which subnational units to belong to, in order to give meaning to notions of self-rule, self-determination, ownership and autonomy. That is why the referendums on the creation of new subnational units in Ghana and Ethiopia, for example, are significant. In Ghana, referendums held in December 2018 led to the creation of six new regions from the existing ten (new regions emerged from Brong Ahafo, Northern, Volta and Western regions, while Ashanti, Central, Eastern, Greater Accra, Upper East and Upper West were left intact). The high percentages (99–99.7 per cent) of 'yes' votes in favour of the new regions gave some indication of people's strong desire to have their 'own states'. The need for people to have a say in where they belong at the subnational level cannot, therefore, be overemphasised.

SHARED RULE

Let us then turn to the supposedly more difficult issues, beginning with that of shared rule, which requires a reasonable degree of devolution of power and local autonomy. Without a doubt, the dominant response to this has been decentralisation, a situation that has given rise to what Erk (2014) describes as 'suddenly emerging new species of massively decentralizing states in Africa' noting, with an obvious tinge of exaggeration, that 'the entire sub-Saharan Africa almost in unison has become decentralized'. Decentralisation – which involves transfer of authority, powers, resources and responsibilities from central governments to lower or subordinate levels, resulting in some measure of local autonomy – has long been recognised as a federal instrumentality, and is certainly not new or 'suddenly emerging' in Africa. Most constitutions, like that of Kenya (2010, article 174), list the objects of devolution to include fostering national unity by recognising diversity; giving powers of self-governance to the people and enhancing their participation in the exercise of powers of the state and in making decisions that affect them; recognising the right of communities to manage their own affairs; and ensuring equitable sharing of national and local resources. The objects clearly articulate federal principles, but the problem is that decentralisation has not worked well, having produced more deconcentration and delegation than devolution, and more potential and promise than delivery on set goals – all for the simple reason that the central state will just not let go. Yet, properly done, decentralisation and local self-governance can be remedies for the failure of the centralised state (see the contributions in Wunsch and Olowu, 1990), and also serve as federal and consociational instrumentalities for refounding the state (Wunsch, 2000). This requires, at a minimum, that local groups have the resources to actually rule themselves and participate actively in shared governance with higher orders, in what Olowu and Wunsch (2004) call 'democratic decentralization'. Wunsch (2000: 487) elaborates further:

> [there has to be] space for local leaders to lead local institutional development, authority to play a role in national governance, a process to develop consensus on central policy, and to check the centre when there is no consensus. This requires a foundation of viable, real, developed structures of local governance if it is to succeed.

From this characterisation, the nature and capacity of decentralisation required to refound the state is more substantial than is offered by those forms of the 'suddenly emerging' decentralisation that have been trending since the 1990s. There are at least three reasons why suddenly emerging decentralisation schemes cannot fit the bill. First is that they are undertaken at the behest and discretion of central governments, meaning that central governments remain the only determinate governments and can recentralise at will. This falls short of the federal complexion of decentralisation that guarantees and institutionalises local autonomy as a safeguard against the overbearing powers of central governments – discretionary decentralisation is unitarist (Osaghae, 1990). Secondly, the schemes have mostly been designed and delivered – in many instances imposed as conditionalities tied to aid – by donors and development partners as part of reform packages, rather than as self-generating responses to local impulses and demands for state reconfiguration. Moreover, they stem from diagnoses that seek to isolate governance deficits, weak institutions, revenue mobilisation and service delivery from their historical contexts, and neglect the more fundamental and debilitating questions of state legitimacy and collective ownership. By making central governments the drivers, donor-authored decentralisation reforms reinforce the top-down configurations referred to earlier. This indeed works for weakened central states that have embraced the 'rhetoric and institutions of decentralization' to subvert subnational institutions and increase their powers (Suberu, 2013: 27; also Boone, 2003).

Cameroon's decision to 'decentralise' some of its powers in 2019 is a good example of this, as it offered the adamant central government the expedient option of autonomy demanded by Anglophone separatists. Thirdly, decentralisation is designed and applied as one-size-fits-all uniform models to all localities, with scant regard for historical, cultural or religious differences and peculiarities. A federal solution requires a more nuanced and contextual approach that is able to address local demands. For these reasons, it is not surprising that after over three decades, decentralisation has failed to produce meaningful changes as a state-rebuilding instrumentality – in fact, it has restored and increased the allocative powers of central governments, which were already declining. Most evaluations note the failure of decentralisation to improve governance, accountability, and resource access and use (see, for example, Bierschenk and Olivier de Sardon, 2003, on powers of the village in Benin). Of the four criteria used to evaluate decentralisation in 10 countries (Botswana, Ghana, Burkina Faso, Mozambique, Mali, Ethiopia, Nigeria, South Africa, Tanzania and Uganda) – viz. legal authority, autonomy, accountability and capacity – Dickovick and Wunsch (2014) found that legal authority scored highest, largely because it posed no real threat to the central state, which anyway had several other top-down exertions and historical legacies (fiscal allocation, dominant political parties, control over local elections and deployment of officials) to emasculate local autonomy.

None of this diminishes the importance of decentralisation as a key federal solution to state rebuilding. It promotes local self-governance and ownership, encourages exchanges and reciprocities among orders of government, and provides a basis for shared governance in terms of local participation in national governance, as Wunsch has so well characterised it. Decentralisation should be able to leverage the established communitarian traditions of autonomy and self-help that underlie, for example, the autonomous communities of the Igbo of south-eastern Nigeria and the 'historical collective choice institutions' of autonomous local units in Somaliland (Dickovick and Wunsch, 2014: 7). This cannot be if the local units are not organic, and if peoples and groups have no say in their constitution. In this regard, a useful model is offered by the multi-layered panchayati system of local government in India, Pakistan, Sri Lanka, Bangladesh and Nepal, which is built on long histories of local autonomy from the village level to higher local orders, and which offers local communities their own spaces for development. Ethiopia's multi-tier local government system, which allocates revenue sources, and statutory powers and responsibilities at the zone, special *woreda* and *woreda kebele* levels, comes closest to the *panchayati*. Regassa (2009: 62) believes that with these provisions of recognition, 'the distinct identity and powers of local government institutions [in Ethiopia] are rendered indestructible'. The constitutionally guaranteed autonomy of local governments in Nigeria and South Africa, which have enumerated legislative competences, taxing powers and elected governance structures, and which require constitutional amendments for any change, are also notable in this regard (although South Africa's local governance is geared more towards efficient service delivery than accommodating diversity). The overall point is that decentralisation cannot serve the purpose of rebuilding the state if it is done at the discretion of central states. Also, for as long as subnational units do not have independent sources of revenue and have to depend on discretionary – and discriminatory – allocations from central governments, decentralisation, local autonomy and local self-governance cannot be meaningful, and the units will simply remain channels for the distribution of centrally controlled resources, rather than centres of growth and productivity, given the overemphasis on equity and distributive justice that justifies and reinforces the need for central control.

RESOURCE CONTROL

We turn next to issues of resource control. One of the lasting legacies of colonialism for the state, and a major source of tension and conflict, is the management and control of resources, who owns and gets what, when and how. This underlies agitations over the control of resources and the huge revenues and other benefits that come with them – agitations that represent some of the most disruptive and pervasive manifestations of state failure. The logic of extraction which drove the colonial enterprise and state economic policies saw the expropriation of resources (land, minerals and agricultural commodities) and dispossession of the people who owned them. The logic was reinforced by the nationalisation policies by which many countries (Mali, Zambia, Ethiopia, Tanzania, Uganda, Sierra Leone, Zaire, Togo, Zimbabwe, Mozambique, Ghana, Kenya) took over control of copper, gold, diamond and iron mines, oil fields, plantations and other major revenue-yielding industries (Rood, 1976). Although these policies are no longer fashionable – thanks to structural adjustment and neoliberal reforms, which have brought the private sector and foreign investors back in – states nevertheless retain control of the economy, and especially of the main revenue-yielding oil and gas, diamonds, iron, gold, uranium, copper, etc. However, what is most remarkable about these resources and the benefits accruing from them is that the groups, communities and peoples of the resource-bearing lands – those who, in most African cultures and customary practices, are regarded as 'owners' – are completely missing from the transactions with either the state or the foreign multinationals. This is despite the huge ecological costs that come with exploration, mining and other activities. In the case of multinationals, the best the communities ever got were non-mandatory corporate social responsibility projects and, in some cases, payment for the lease or sale of land.

This has been the lot of copper-mining communities in Zambia, even though the Mines and Mineral Development Act of 2015 provides for development agreements on local content and promotion of local businesses (Werner, 2016). The situation is pretty much the same all over the continent. For their part, central governments collect the rents, royalties and other revenues, while – with varying degrees of discretion – giving little or nothing to the resource 'owners'. Nigeria was, for a long time, the exception here, as resource-bearing units were compensated with 'derivation' allocations based on contributions to the federation account; but even this is regarded as unsatisfactory and unjust by the oil-bearing Niger Delta minorities. It is on these bases that resource wars have erupted all over Africa, as resource-bearing communities have insisted on 'ownership rights' that range from outright control to adequate derivation rights in shared control with the central state. These wars are a symptom of state failure, to the extent that the roots of expropriation lie deep in the colonial state, although it took diminishing resources and descent into economic insolvency to provoke these dramatic contestations and rejections of that state. In Sierra Leone, Liberia, DR Congo, Central African Republic, Nigeria and other countries, 'gold-digging' warlords (metaphorically speaking), militias and rebel forces hijacked the process; but it would be misleading, on this basis, to reduce the conflicts to mere 'greed and grievance' and 'resource curse' factors: they emanate from foundational and structural problems.

We shall take the case of the struggles by the Bakweri people of Cameroon to regain control of their fertile lands, which were expropriated under German colonial rule and remained in the hands of the Cameroonian government after independence. The case became celebrated when, in October 2002, having exhausted local remedies, the Bakweri Land Claims Committee, on behalf of the minority indigenous community, took the unprecedented step of litigation at the African Commission on Human and People' Rights (ACHPR). Africa's highest human rights tribunal) to 'assert permanent sovereignty over ancestral land' used by the state through the Cameroon Development Corporation (CDC), which was up for privatisation (Kofele-Kale, 2007). Among other things, the Bakweri demanded to be fully involved in CDC privatisation negotiations to protect their interests as owners of the land, to be paid ground rents owed to the dispossessed indigenes dating back to 1947, and to be allocated percentage shares in the privatised companies, in addition to representation on policy and management boards. Although the ACHPR declared the suit inadmissible on the grounds of non-exhaustion of domestic remedies, the Bakweri case showed that the days of excluding resource owners were over, and it is instructive that the ACHPR undertook to use its good offices to ensure that the contending parties reached an amicable resolution.

This is where federalism comes in, the whole purpose of resource struggles being to force the central state to negotiate with resource-bearing groups and grant them a share of the benefits of the resources. And things are changing along these lines in a number of countries. We have already referred to the case of Nigeria, where the principle of derivation is used to allocate a percentage (13 per cent since 1999) of oil revenues to oil-bearing areas (in addition, there are allocations from a special ecological fund to compensate for environmental problems of mining and other exploration activities). Not only has DR Congo adopted the derivation formula that allows provinces to retain 40 per cent of national revenues derived from their territories, but the 2006 constitution also established an equalisation fund to redistribute up to 10 per cent of national revenues to develop infrastructure in poorer provinces.

South Africa has also had its fair share of 'restorative justice'. This has involved an historic benefit-sharing agreement among the government, representatives of the San and Khoi peoples and farming groups that gives the indigenous people who grow, harvest, ferment or dry rooibos 1.5 per cent of the annual revenues of the processors of rooibos tea, in recognition of the traditional knowledge they have held for nearly two centuries. In addition, local small-scale rooibos farmers in the Western and Northern Cape provinces were to henceforth enjoy financial support. All this came after demands by the San and Khoi for compensation for their contribution to the commercialisation of rooibos tea, and followed negotiations with government and commercial groups that lasted for 10 years. To round up, what these interventions and other developments show is that resource wars are not inevitable if central states can negotiate with resource-bearing communities in a manner that recognises their rights to resources and, following that, adequate compensation. It only remains to emphasise that benefit-sharing in favour of resource-bearing groups does not obviate the role of the central state as an agent of balanced development, redistribution and distributive justice – a point that is also central to the philosophy of federalism that all component groups, rich and poor alike, should benefit from the common wealth of the country. But doing so requires cooperation and bargaining, because of the multiple centres of growth and development. When the state refuses to do this, it encourages exclusionary tendencies on the part of members of resource-bearing groups, who feel unjustly treated (as has been the case in Cameroon, Uganda and Angola).

CONCLUSIONS

Africa is rapidly emerging as one of the most important experimental fields for the theory and practice of federalism, and this paper shows why a strictly legal-constitutional approach to the subject is too limited to reap the benefits on offer: a much more nuanced and liberal sociological approach is required. Taking the juncture of state failure in Africa, itself a victim of a false universal that rejects states that deviate from received paradigms as a point of departure, this paper shows that federal solutions offer the relevant framework and principles for rebuilding the state as a decolonial construct of collective ownership, shared rule and self-rule.

The central argument is that the unravelling of the received state, whose failure is manifest in the contestations, conflicts and wars, and overall inability to function as a state, provides the opportunity for renegotiating and re-bargaining the state. This is done within the framework of what I call later-state federalism, which – unlike inception-state federalism, where the central state is constructed from below – is constrained by the enormous powers of the central state, which constructs from above. The objective is not to evaluate the workings of federalism (which is certainly not a magic wand), but to examine how the opportunities it offers as a system of continuous bargain can be optimised and made more enduring.

Nigeria's National Assembly in the federal capital city of Abuja, May 2018. Photo: Runcie Chidebe, Wikimedia Commons

ACKNOWLEDGEMENTS

This paper would be incomplete without reference to the memory of Professor Claude Ake, in whose honour the Claude Ake Chair was jointly instituted by the Department of Peace and Conflict of Uppsala University and the Nordic Africa Institute. I feel privileged to be the holder of the Chair for 2019, and thank Uppsala University and NAI for finding me worthy of the appointment. Although Professor Ake was not a student of federalism, the issues treated in this paper were not only of interest to him, but were germane to his thoughts on transforming the state in Africa to make it better able to deliver on the challenges of human security and development. He considered decolonisation and restructuring of the political economy key tools for this, and this aligns very closely with the interrogations in this paper. I will forever cherish his invitation and encouragement to elaborate on a paper I presented at a conference at the University of Ibadan in 1992 on the management of ethnicity in Africa, which his Centre for Advanced Social Science later published as a monograph (Osaghae, 1994). That monograph became one of the deep wells from which I drew many of my later thoughts. May Professor Ake's departed soul continue to rest in peace. I have had a very good and productive time in Uppsala – as I did in 1994, when I first visited – thanks to the warmth and support of the good people I have had the privilege to meet and work with. For this, I thank all colleagues and friends at NAI and Uppsala University, especially the following: Marie Karlsson, Anders Themnér, Tania Berger, Peter Wallensteen, Therese Sjömander Magnusson, Victor Adetula, Helena Millroth, Redie Bereketeab, Mattias Sköld, Henrik Angerbrandt, Henrik Alfredsson, Camilla Leetmaa, Erik Melander, Kajsa Hallberg Adu, Liisa Laakso, Julia Falkerby, Johan Sävström, Sten Hagberg, Bose Babatunde, Lauren Paramoer, Ronald Ndesanjo and Valence Meriki. Finally, my thanks to my wife Veronica, daughter Osahon and grandchildren Eyitayo and Tamilore for making Uppsala a place of memories to cherish.

BIBLIOGRAPHY

Adamolekun, L. and Kincaid, J. (1991) 'The Federal Solution: An Assessment and Prognosis of Nigeria and Africa', *Publius*, Vol. 21, no. 4

Agbese, P.O. and Kieh, G.K. Jr., eds (2007) *Reconstituting the State in Africa* (New York: Palgrave Macmillan)

Ake, C. (1987) *Revolutionary Pressure in Africa* (London: Zed)

Ayoade, J.A.A. (1988) 'States without Citizens: An Emerging African Phenomenon', in D. Rothchild and N. Chazan, eds, *The Precarious Balance: The State and Society in Africa* (Boulder: Westview)

Bangura, Y. (1995) 'The Pitfalls of Recolonization: A Comment on the Mazrui-Mafeje Exchange', *CODESRIA Bulletin*, no. 4

Bates, R.H. (2008) *When Things Fall Apart: State Failure in Late Twentieth Century Africa* (Cambridge: Cambridge University Press)

Bayart, J. (1991) 'Finishing with the Idea of the Third World: The Concept of the Political Trajectory', in J. Manor, ed., *Rethinking Third World Politics* (London: Longman)

Bayart, J. (1992) 'The Historicity of African Societies', *Journal of International Affairs*, vol. 46, no. 2

Bierschenk, T. and Olivier de Sardon, J. (2003) 'Powers in the Village: Rural Benin between Democratization and Decentralization', *African Affairs*, vol. 73, no. 2

Boas, M. and Jennings, K. (2007) '"Failed States" and "State Failure": Threats or Opportunities', *Globalization*, vol. 4, no. 4

Boone, C. (2003) 'Decentralization as Political Strategy in West Africa', *Comparative Political Studies*, vol. 36, no. 4

Burgess, M. (2012a) *In Search of the Federal Spirit* (Oxford: Oxford University Press)

Burgess M. (2012b) "Multinational Federalism in Multinational Federation", in M. Seymour and AG Gagnon, eds. *Multinational Federalism. The Comparative Territorial Politics series* (London: Palgrave Macmillan)

Busia, K. (1967) *Africa in Search of Democracy* (London: Routledge & Kegan Paul)

Chabal, P. and Daloz, J. (1999) *Africa Works: Disorder as Political Instrument* (London: International African Institute; Bloomington, Indiana University Press)

Chanie, P. (2007) 'Clientelism and Ethiopia's Post-1991 Decentralization', *Journal of Modern African Studies*, vol. 45, no. 3

Chesterman, S. et al., eds, *Making States Work: State Failure and the Crisis of Governance* (Tokyo: United Nations University Press)

Clapham, C. (2001) "Rethinking African States", *African Security Review*, vol. 10, no 3

Clapham, C. (2011) "Africa and Trusteeship in the Modern Global Order", in J. Mayall and R.S. de Oliveira, ed. *The new Protectorates: International Tutelage and the Making of Liberal States* (New York: Columbia University Press)

Dent, M. (1989) 'Federalism in Africa, with Special Reference to Nigeria', in M. Forsyth, ed., *Federalism and Nationalism* (Leicester & London: Leicester University Press)

Dickovick, J.T. and Wunsch, J.S., eds (2014) *Decentralization in Africa: The Paradox of State Strength* (Boulder: Lynne Rienner)

Dudley, B.J. (1966) 'Federalism and the Balance of Political Power in Nigeria', *Journal of Commonwealth Political Studies*, Vol. 4

Eisenstadt, S.N., Abitbol, M. and Chazan, N., eds (1988) *The Early State in African Perspective: Culture, Power and Division of Labour* (Leiden and New York: E.J. Brill)

Ekeh, P.P. (1983) *Colonialism and Social Structure in Africa: An Inaugural Lecture* (Ibadan: Ibadan University Press)

Ellis, S. (2005) 'How to Rebuild Africa', *Foreign Affairs*, vol. 84, no. 5

Englebert, P. (1997) 'The Contemporary African State: Neither African nor State', *Third World Quarterly*, vol. 18, no. 4

Erk, J. (2014) 'Federalism and Decentralization in Sub-Saharan Africa: Five Patterns of Evolution', *Regional and Federal Studies*, vol. 24, no. 5

Erk, J. and Swenden, W. eds. (2010) *New Directions in Federalism Studies* (London: Routledge)

Fessha, Y.T. (2010) *Ethnic Diversity and Federalism: Constitution Making in South Africa and Ethiopia* (Surrey: Ashgate)

Fiseha, A. (2012) 'Ethiopia's Experiment in Accommodating Diversity: 20 Years Balance Sheet', *Regional and Federal Studies*, vol. 22, no. 4

Gana, A.T. and Egwu, S., eds (2003) *Federalism in Africa. Vol. 1: Framing the National Question* (Trenton: Africa World Press)

Geertz, C. (1963) 'The Integration Revolution', in *Old Societies and New States* (Glencoe: The Free Press, 1963)

Geshiere, P. (2013) 'Autochthony and the Politics of Belonging', in N. Cheeseman, D.M. Anderson and A. Scheibler, eds, *Routledge Handbook of African Politics* (London and New York: Routledge)

Habtu, A. (2005) 'Multiethnic Federalism in Ethiopia: A Study of the Secession Clause in Constitution', *Publius*, vol. 24, no. 5

Hazlewood, A. (1967) *African Integration and Disintegration: Case Studies in Economic and Political Union* (London: Oxford University Press)

Heilbrunn, J.R. (1993) 'Social Origins of National Conferences in Benin and Togo', *Journal of Modern African Studies*, vol. 31, no. 2

Helman, G.B. and Ratner, S.R. (1992–93) 'Saving Failed States', *Foreign Policy*, no. 89

Herbst, J. (2000) *States and Power in Africa: Comparative Lessons in Authority and Control* (Princeton: Princeton University Press)

Herbst, J. (2004) 'Let Them Fail: State Failure in Theory and Practice', in R.I. Rotberg, ed., *When States Fail: Causes and Consequences* (Princeton: Princeton University Press)

Herbst, J. and Mills, G. (2006) 'Africa's Big Dysfunctional States: An Introductory Overview', in C. Clapham et al., eds, *Big African States* (Johannesburg: Wits University Press)

Horowitz, D. (2007) 'The Many Uses of Federalism', *Drake Law Review*, vol. 55

Hueglin, T.O. and Fenna, A. (2015) *Comparative Federalism: A Systematic Inquiry* (Toronto: University of Toronto Press)

Hyden, G. (1980) *Beyond Ujamaa in Tanzania: Underdevelopment and Uncaptured Peasantry* (London: Heinemann)

Jackson, R.H. and Rosberg, C.G. (1982) "Why Africa's Weak States Persist: The Empirical and Juridical in Statehood", *World Politics*, vol. 35, no 1

Kimenyi, M.S. (1997) *Ethnic Diversity, Liberty and the State: The Africa Dilemma* (Cheltenham: Edward Elgar)

Kofele-Kale, N. (2007) 'Asserting Permanent Sovereignty over Ancestral Lands: The Bakweri Land Litigation against Cameroon', *Annual Survey of International and Comparative Law*, vol. 13, no. 1

Kothari, R. (1988) *State Against Democracy: In Search of Humane Governance*

(Delhi: Ajanta Publications)

Kuperman, A.J., ed. (2015) *Constitutions and Conflict Management in Africa: Preventing Civil War through Constitutional Design* (Philadelphia: University of Pennsylvania Press)

Kymlicka, W. (2006) "Emerging Western Models of Multination Federalism: Are they Relevant for Africa?", in D. Turton, ed. *Ethnic Federalism: The Ethiopian Experience in Comparative Perspective* (Oxford: James Currey)

Lewis, P.M. and Harbeson, J.W., eds (2016) *Coping with Crisis in African States* (Boulder: Lynne Rienner)

Lijphart, A. (1985) 'Non-Majoritarian Democracy: A Comparison of Federal and Consociational Theories', *Publius*, vol. 15, no. 2

Livingston, W.S. (1952) 'A Note on the Nature of Federalism', *Political Science Quarterly*, vol. 67, no. 1

Mafeje, A. (1995) 'Benign Recolonization and Malignant Minds in the Service of Imperialism', *CODESRIA Bulletin*, no 2

Mafeje, A. (1998) 'The Beast and the Icon: No End to Ali Mazrui's Pax-Africana Muddles', *CODESRIA Bulletin*, no 2

Mamdani, M. (1997) *Citizen and Subject: Contemporary Africa and the Legacy of Late Colonialism* (Princeton: Princeton University Press)

Mazrui, A. (1995) 'Self-Colonization and the Search for Pax-Africana: A Rejoinder', *CODESRIA Bulletin*, no. 2

McHenry, D E. 1997. Federalism in Africa: Is it a Solution to, or a Cause of, Ethnic Problems? Paper read at the annual African Studies Association Conference, Columbus, Ohio

McKown, R. (1988) 'Federalism in Africa', in C.L. Brown-John, ed., *Centralizing and Decentralizing Trends in Federal States* (Lanham: University Press of America)

Menkhaus, K. and Shapiro, J.N. (2010) 'Non-State Actors and Failed States: Lessons from Al-Qaida's Experiences in the Horn of Africa', in A.L. Clunan and H.A. Trinkunas, eds, *Ungoverned Spaces: Alternatives to State Authority in an Era of Softened Sovereignty* (Stanford: Stanford Security Studies)

Ndlovu-Gatsheni, S.J. (2015) *Coloniality of Power in Postcolonial Africa: Myths of Decolonization* (Dakar: CODESRIA Books)

Newman, E. (2007) 'Weak States, State Failure and Terrorism', *Terrorism and Political Studies*, vol. 19, no. 4

Nwajiaku, K. (1994) 'The National Conferences in Benin and Togo Revisited', *Journal of Modern African Studies*, vol. 32, no. 3

Nzongola-Ntalaja, G. (1987) *Revolution and Counterrevolution in Africa: Essays in Contemporary Politics* (London: Zed)

Olowu, D. and Wunsch, J., eds (2004) *Local Governance in Africa: The Challenges of Democratic Decentralization* (Boulder: Lynne Rienner)

Osaghae, E.E. (1986) 'On the Concept of the Ethnic Group in Africa: A Nigerian Case', *Plural Societies*, vol. xvi, no. 2

Osaghae, E.E. (1990) 'A Reassessment of Federalism as a Degree of Decentralization', Publius: *The Journal of Federalism*, vol. 20, no. 1

Osaghae, E.E. (1994) *Ethnicity and its Management in Africa: The Democratization Link* (Lagos and Oxford: Malthouse, for Centre for Advanced Social Science)

Osaghae, E.E. (1997) 'The Federal Solution in Comparative Perspective', *Politeia*, vol. 16, no. 1

Osaghae, E.E. (1998) 'Managing Multiple Minority Problems in a Divided Society: The Nigerian Experience', *Journal of Modern African Studies*, vol. 36, no. 1

Osaghae, E.E. (2000) 'Rescuing the Post-Colonial State in Africa: A Reconceptualization of the Role of Civil Society', *International Journal of African Studies*, vol. 2, no. 1

Osaghae, E.E. (2004a) "Political Transitions and Ethnic Conflict in Africa", *Journal of Third World Studies*, vol. 21, no 1

Osaghae, E.E. (2004b) "Federalism and the Management of Diversity in Africa", *Identity, Culture and Politics*, vol. 5, nos. 1 & 2

Osaghae, E.E. (2005a) "State, Constitutionalism and the Management of Ethnicity in Africa", *Asian and African Studies*, vol. 4, nos. 1 & 2

Osaghae, E.E. (2005b) "The State of Africa's Second Liberation", *Interventions: International Journal of Postcolonial Studies*, vol. 7

Osaghae, E.E. (2007) 'Fragile States', *Development in Practice*, vol. 17, nos 4 & 5

Osaghae, E.E. (2019) *What Man has Joined Together: Ethnicity, Federalism and State Politics, University of Ibadan Inaugural Lecture* (Ibadan: Ibadan University Press)

Osaghae, E.E. (2020) 'Africa in the Throes of Global Pushes and Pulls', in K.P. Coleman, M. Kornprobst and A. Seegers, eds, *Diplomacy and Borderlands: African Agency at the Intersections of Orders* (London and New York: Routledge)

Owusu, M. (1983) "Chieftaincy and Constitutionalism in Ghana: The Case of the Third Republic", *Studies in Third World Societies*, vol. 24, no 2

Peters, B. Guy (1999) *Institutional Theory in Political Science: The 'New Institutionalism'*, (London: Pinter)

Pierson, Paul (2000) 'The Limits of Design: Explaining Institutional Origins and Change', *Governance*, vol. 13, no. 4

Ramphal, S. (1979) 'Keynote Address', in A.B. Akinyemi, P.D. Cole and W. Ofonagoro, eds, *Readings on Federalism* (Lagos: Macmillan and Nigerian Institute of International Affairs)

Regassa, T. (2009) 'Sub-National Constitutions in Ethiopia: Towards Entrenching Constitutionalism at State Level', *Mizan Law Review*, vol. 3, no. 1

Rood, L.L. (1976) 'Nationalization and Indigeneity in Africa', *Journal of Modern African Studies*, vol. 14, no. 3

Rotberg, R.I. (2004) 'The Failure and Collapse of Nation-States: Breakdown, Prevention and Repair', in R.I. Rotberg, ed., *When States Fail: Causes and Consequences* (Princeton: Princeton University Press)

Rothchild, D. (1997) *Managing Ethnic Conflict in Africa* (Washington: Brookings Institution Press)

Rothchild, D. (1999) 'Ethnic Insecurity, Peace Agreements and State Building', in R. Joseph, ed., State, *Conflict and Democracy in Africa* (Boulder: Lynne Rienner)

Scott, C. (2017) *State Failure in Sub-Saharan Africa: The Crisis of Post-Colonial Order* (London: I.B. Tauris)

Sklar, R. (1993) 'The African Frontier for Political Science', in R.H. Bates, V.Y. Mudimbe and J. O'Barr, eds, *Africa and the Disciplines: The Contributions of Research in Africa to the Social Sciences and Humanities* (Chicago and London: University of Chicago Press)

Sklar, R. (1999) 'The Significance of Mixed Studies in Southern Africa Studies: A Preliminary Assessment', in J. Hyslop, ed., *Always Something New: African Democracy in the Era of Globalization* (Johannesburg: Wits University Press)

Smock, D.R. and Bentsi-Enchill, K., eds (1976) *The Search for National Integration in Africa* (New York: Free Press)

Steinmo, S., Thelen, K. and Longstreth, F., eds (1992) *Structuring Politics: Historical Institutionalism in Comparative Analysis* (Cambridge: Cambridge University Press)

Stren, R. and Eyoh, D. (2007) 'Decentralization and Urban Development in West Africa', in D. Eyoh and R. Stren, eds, *Decentralization and Urban Development in West Africa* (Washington: Woodrow Wilson International Centre for Scholars)

Suberu, R.T. (2013) 'Federalism and Decentralization', in N. Cheeseman, D.M. Anderson and A. Scheibler, eds, *Routledge Handbook of African Politics* (London and New York: Routledge)

Thomas-Woolley, B. and Keller E. (1994) 'Majority Rule and Minority Rights: American Federalism and African Experience', *Journal of Modern African Studies*, vol. 32, no. 3

Veenendaal, W.P. (2015) 'Origins and Persistence of Federalism and Decentralization in Microstates', *Publius*, vol. 45, no. 4

Watts, R.L. (2013) 'Typologies of Federalism', in *Routledge Handbook of Regionalism and Federalism* (New York: Routledge)

Weaver, K. and Rockman, S., eds (1993) *Do Institutions Matter? Government Capabilities in the United States and Abroad* (Washington: Brookings Institution)

Werner, K. (2016) 'Zambia: Governance and Natural Resources', *Revue Governance*, vol. 13, no. 2

Wheare, K.C. (1967) *Federal Government* (London and New York: Oxford University Press)

Wiredu, K. (1996) *Cultural Universals and Particulars* (Bloomington: Indiana University Press)

Wunsch, J.S. (2000) 'Refounding the African State and Local Self-Governance: The Neglected Foundation', *Journal of Modern African Studies*, vol. 38, no. 3

Wunsch, J.S. (2014) "Decentralization: Theoretical, Conceptual and Analytical Issues", in J.T. Dickovick and J.S. Wunsch, J.S., eds. *Decentralization in Africa: The Paradox of State Strength* (Boulder: Lynne Rienner)

Wunsch, J.S. and Olowu, D., eds (1990) *The Failure of the Centralized State: Institutions and Self-Governance in Africa* (Boulder: Westview)

THE CLAUDE AKE MEMORIAL PAPER

The Claude Ake Visiting Chair, set up in 2003 by the Department of Peace and Conflict Research, Uppsala University (DPCR) and the Nordic Africa Institute (NAI) with funding from the Swedish government and Uppsala University, honours the memory of Professor Claude Ake (1939-1996), a Nigerian political scientist. It is intended for scholars who, like him, combine a profound commitment to scholarship with a strong advocacy for social justice. The visiting chair holder is offered a conducive environment in Uppsala to pursue his or her own research. Based on the research they pursue while in Uppsala, the holders of the Claude Ake Visiting Chair give a public lecture, which, in a general sense, relates to the work of Claude Ake. The lecture is based on a paper that is subsequently published jointly by DPCR and NAI in the Claude Ake Memorial Paper (CAMP) series. Below is a list of previous titles in the series:

1. JINADU, L. Adele; Explaining and Managing Ethnic Conflict in Africa: Towards a Cultural Theory of Democracy (2007)

2. OBI, Cyril I.; No Choice, But Democracy: Prising the People out of Politics in Africa? (2008)

3. SESAY, Amadu; The African Union: Forward March or About Face-Turn? (2008)

4. BOAFO-ARTHUR, Kwame; Democracy and Stability in West Africa: The Ghanaian Experience (2008)

5. VILLA-VICENCIO, Charles; Where the Old Meets the New: Transitional Justice, Peacebuilding and Traditional Reconciliation Practices in Africa (2009)

6. MOHAMED, Adam Azzain; Evaluating the Darfur Peace Agreement: A Call for an Alternative Approach to Crisis Management (2009)

7. MBABAZI, Pamela K; The Oil Industry in Uganda: A Blessing in Disguise or an all Too Familiar Curse? (2013)

8. ADETULA, Victor A.O.; African Conflicts, Development and Regional Organisations in the Post-Cold War International System (2015)

9. GOBODO-MADIKIZELA, Pumla; What Does It Mean to be Human in the Aftermath of Historical Trauma? Re-envisioning The Sunflower and Why Hannah Arendt was Wrong (2016)

10. MURITHI, Tim; Regional Reconciliation in Africa: The Elusive Dimension of Peace and Security (2019)

11. HUDSON, Heidi, A (Wo)man for all seasons: Amos Tutuola and the Gendering of Peace in Africa (2019)

All titles can be downloaded in full text at the NAI web site www.nai.uu.se.